STUDIES IN
CHRISTIAN EDUCATION

EDUCATIONAL EXPERIENCES BEFORE THE MIDNIGHT CRY

COMPARED WITH

EDUCATIONAL EXPERIENCES BEFORE THE LOUD CRY.

BY E. A. SUTHERLAND

"Now as never before we need to understand the true science of education. If we fail to understand this we shall never have a place in the Kingdom of God."

—MRS E. G. WHITE.

TEACH Services, Inc.
New York

Facsimile Reproduction

As this book played a formative role in the development of Christian thought
and the publisher feels that this book, with its candor and depth, still holds
significance for the church today. Therefore the publisher has chosen to
reproduce this historical classic from an original copy. Frequent variations in
the quality of the print are unavoidable due to the condition of the original.
Thus the print may look darker or lighter or appear to be missing detail, more
in some places than in others.

2005   05   06   07   08   09   10   11   12   · 5   4   3   2   1

Copyright © 2005 TEACH Services, Inc.
ISBN 1-57258-299-5
Library of Congress Catalog Card No. 2004111822

Published by
TEACH Services, Inc.
www.TEACHServices.com

Contents

Foreward

The Students' Volunteer Band of the NASHVILLE AGRI-CULTURAL AND NORMAL INSTITUTE had the privilege of listening to a course of lectures delivered by Doctor E. A. Sutherland, setting forth the fact that the great Protestant denominations failed to give the first angel's message in its fulness because they did not free themselves from the Papal system of education. They clung to this system, and it finally brought them to its own level, thus making them Babylon.

The Seventh-day Adventist denomination came into existence because of this failure, and they must succeed where the others failed. Their birthright is a great reform movement, the greatest the world has ever known. The Lord has been telling our people that we as individuals are in positive danger of suffering the same defeat as they, because we are still clinging to worldly methods of education. They failed to give the midnight cry because of their wrong education. We as young people believe that we are about to enter upon the period of the latter rain. From these lectures we know that any Seventh-day Adventist who is linked up with worldly education can have no part in the loud cry. We trust the following pages may be earnestly and prayerfully read, and that they may do for you what they have done for us.

THE PRICE OF THIS PAMPHLET IS 25c THE COPY, but it is sent free to any one who requests it. If the reading helps you, and you realize that others will be benefitted by reading it also, and you are disposed to assist in its distribution, a contribution to our literature fund will be very much appreciated. Such contributions may be sent to the Students' Volunteer Band, N. A. & N. Institute, Madison, Tenn.

BEGINNING OF THE EDUCATIONAL HISTORY IN THE UNITED STATES.

THAT CHURCH TRIUMPHS which breaks the yoke of worldly education, and which develops and practices the principles of Christian education.

"Now, as never before, we need to understand the true science of education. If we fail to understand this we shall never have a place in the kingdom of God." (U. T., July 8, 1897). "The science of true education is the truth. The third angel's message is truth." (T. Vol. 6, p. 131). It is taken for granted that. all Seventh-day Adventists believe that Christian education and the third angel's message are the same truth. The two are as inseparable as are a tree's roots and its trunk and branches.

The object of these studies is to give a better understanding of the reason for the decline and moral fall of the Protestant denominations at the time of the midnight cry in 1844, and to help us as Seventh-day Adventists to avoid their mistakes as we approach the loud cry, soon due to the world.

A BRIEF SURVEY of the history of the Protestant denominations shows that their spiritual downfall in 1844 was the result of their failure "to understand the true science of education." Their failure to understand and to practice Christian education unfitted them to proclaim to the world the message of Christ's second coming. The Seventh-day Adventist demonination was then called into existence to take up the work which the popular churches had failed to train their missionaries to do. The Protestant denominations could not give the third angel's message, a reform movement, which is a warning against the beast and his image, because they were still clinging to those doctrines and those principles of education which themselves form the beast and his image. It is important that young Seventh-day Adventists study seriously the causes of the spiritual decline of these churches in 1844, lest we repeat their history, and be cast aside the Spirit of God, and thus lose our place in the kingdom. If Seventh-day Adventists succeed where they failed, we must have a system of education which repudiates those principles which in themselves develop the beast and his image. "Now, all these things happened unto them for ensamples; and they are written for our admonition upon whom the ends of the world are come."

PROTESTANTISM, born in the sixteenth century, was about to lose its light in Europe. God then prepared a new land, the future United States, as a cradle for the protection and development of those principles, and from this country is to go forth the final worldwide message that heralds the Saviour's return.

"It was a desire for liberty of conscience that inspired the Pilgrims to brave the perils of the long journey across the sea, to endure the hardships and dangers of the wilderness, and, with God's blessing, to lay on the shores of America the foundation of a mighty nation... The Bible was held as the foundation of faith, and source of wisdom and the charter of liberty. Its principles were diligently taught in the home, in the school and in the church, and its fruits were manifest in thrift, intelligence, purity and temperance. . . It was demonstrated that the principles of the Bible are the surest safeguards to national greatness." (G. C., p. 292, 296).

THESE REFORMERS, on reaching America, renounced the Papal doctrines in church and state, but they retained the Papal system of education. "While the reformers rejected the creed of Rome, they were not entirely free from her spirit of intolerance. . . The English reformers, while renouncing the doctrines of Romanism, had retained many of its forms." Some "looked upon them as badges of the slavery from which they had been delivered, and to which they had no disposition to return. Many earnestly desired to return to the purity and simplicity which characterized the primitive church. . . England had ceased forever to be a habitable spot. Some at last determined to seek refuge in Holland. Difficulties, losses and imprisonment were encountered. . . In their flight they had left their houses, their goods, their means of livelihood. . . They cheerfully accepted the situation, and lost no time in idleness or repining. They knew they were pilgrims. . . In the midst of exile and hardship their love and faith waxed strong. They trusted the Lord's promises, and He did not fail them in time of need; and when God's hand seemed pointing them across the sea, to a land where they might found for themselves a state and leave to their children the precious heritage of religious liberty, they went forward without shrinking, in the path of Providence. . . The Puritans had joined themselves together by a solemn covenant as the *Lord's free people* to walk in all His ways, made known or to be made known to them. *Here was the true spirit of reform, the vital principle of Protestantism."* G. C., pp. 289 ,293).

THE EDUCATIONAL SYSTEM of the church, which had driven them from their native home, was one of the most serious errors from which the Puritans failed to break away. This system of education, while Papal in spirit, was, to a certain extent, Protestant in form. The historian writes of the schools of the Puritans in the New World, that their courses were "fitted to the time-sanctioned curriculum of the college. They taught much Latin and Greek, an extended course in mathematics, and were strong generally on the side of the humanities. . . This was a modeling after Rugby Eton and other noted English schools." Again we read, "The roots of this system were deep in the great ecclesiastical system." "From his early training," Dunster, one of the first presidents of Harvard, "patterned the Harvard course largely after that of the English Universities." They so faithfully patterned after the English model—Cambridge University—that they were called by that name, and the historian wrote of Harvard, "In several instances youths in the parent country were sent to the *American Cambridge* for a finishing education." Boone, speaking of the courses of study of William and Mary prior to the Revolution, says, "All were of English pattern." Of Yale, started later, it is said, "The regulations for the most part were those at Harvard, as also the courses of study." The younger patterned after the older. It is very natural that Yale should be established after the English Papal system, because the founder, Elihu

Yale, had spent twenty years in the English schools. "Twenty years he spent in the schools and in special study." (Boone, pp. 24-40).

Seventh-day Adventists should not let this fact escape their attention: the three leading schools of the colonies were established by men who had fled from the Papal doctrines of the Old World; but these educators, because of their training in these Papal schools and their ignorance of the relation between education and religion, unwittingly patterned their institutions after the educational system of the church from which they had withdrawn.

It is surprising that these English Reformers, after sacrificing as they did for a worthy cause, should yet allow a system of education, so unfitted to all their purposes, to be in reality the nurse of their children, from whose bosom these children drew their nourishment. They did not realize that the character and Christian experience of these children depended upon the nature of the food received. Had they grasped the relation of the education of the child to the experience of the same individual in the church, they would not have borrowed this Papal system of education, but would have cast it out bodily as too dangerous for tolerance within the limits of Protestantism.

SOME FACTS from educational history will make clear the statement that the system of education in Oxford, Cambridge, Eton and Rugby was Papal, and the New England reformers, patterning their schools after these models, were planting the Papal system of education in America. Laurie says, "Oxford and Cambridge modeled themselves largely after Paris. . . A large number of masters and their pupils left Paris.

. . . Thus the English portion of (Paris) University went to Oxford and Cambridge." The relation of the University of Paris, the mother of Cambridge and Oxford, to the Papacy is thus expressed, "It was because it was the center of theological learning that it received so many privileges from the Pope, and was kept in close relation to the Papal See." (Laurie, pp. 153, 162, 242).

LUTHER AND MELANCTHON, the great sixteenth century reformers, understood clearly that it was mipossible to have a permanent religious reform without Christian education. So they not only gave attention to the doctrines of the Papacy, but also developed a strong system of Christian schools. Melancthon said, "To neglect the young in our schools is just like taking the spring out of the year. They indeed take away the spring from the year who permit the schools to decline, because religion cannot be maintained without them." "Melancthon steadily directed his efforts to the advancement of education and the building up of good Christian schools... In the spring of 1525, with Luther's help, he reorganized the schools of Eisleben and Madgeburg." He declared, "The cause of true education is the cause of God." (Melancthon, p. 81).

"In 1528 Melancthon drew up the 'Saxony School Plan,' which served as the basis of organization for many schools throughout Germany." This plan dealt with the question of a "multiplicity of studies that were not only unfruitful but even hurtful. . . The teacher should not burden the children with too many books." (Painter, p. 152). These reformers realized that the strength of the Papal church lay in its educational system, and they struck a crushing blow at this system and, wounding it, brought the Papal church to her knees. The reformers established a system of Christian schools that made Protestants of the children. This wonderful revolution in education and religion was accomplished in one genreation, in the brief space of one man's life.

To give an idea of the power in that great Christian educational movement, the historian, speaking of several European countries, says: "The nobility of that country studied in Wittenberg—all the colleges of the land were filled with Protestants. . . Not more than the thirtieth part of the population remained Catholic. . . They withheld their children, too, from the Catholic schools. The inhabitants of Maniz did not hesitate to send their children to Protestant schools. The Protestant notions extended their vivifying energies to the most remote and most forgotten corners of Europe. What an immense domain had they conquered within the space of forty years. . . Twenty years had elapsed in Vienna since a single student of the University had taken priests' orders. . . About this period the teachers in Germany were all, almost without exceptions, Protestants. The whole body of the rising generation sat at their feet and imbibed a hatred of the Pope with the first rudiments of learning" (Von Ranke, p. 135).

After the death of Luther and Melancthon, the theologians, into whose hands the work of the Reformation fell, instead of multiplying Christian schools, became absorbed in the mere technicalities of theology, and passed by the greatest work of the age. They sold their birthright for a mess of pottage. When the successors of Luther and Melancthon failed to continue that constructive work, which centered largely in the education of the youth, who were to be the future missionaries and pillars of the church, internal dissention arose. Their time was spent very largely in criticising the views of some of their colaborers who differed with them on some unimportant points of theology. Thus they became destructive instead of constructive. They paid much attention to doctrines, and spent the most of their energy in preserving orthodoxy. They crystallized their doctrines into a creed; they ceased to develop, and lost the spirit of Christian education, which was the oil for their lamps. Protestantism degenerated into dead orthodoxy, and they broke up into opposing factions. The Protestant church, thus weakened, could not resist the great power of rejuvenated Papal education.

THE SUCCESS OF THE REFORMERS had been due to their control of the young people through their educational system. The Papal schools were almost forsaken during the activity of Luther and Melancthon. But when these reformers died and their successors became more interested in abstract theology than in Christian education, and spent their time, energy and the money of the church in preaching and writing on abstract theology, the Papal school system, recovering itself, rose to a life and death struggle with the Protestant church. The Papacy realized that the existence of the Papal church itself depended upon a victory over Protestant schools. We are surprised at the skill and tact the Papal educators used in their attack, and the rapidity with which they gained the victory. This experience should be an object lesson forever to Seventh-day Adventists.

A CHRISTIAN SCHOOL ANIMATED BY THE PAPAL SPIRIT.—The eyes of the successors of Luther and Melancthon were blinded. They did not understand "the true science of education." They did not see its importance, and grasp the dependence of character upon education. "The true object of education is to restore the image of God in the soul." (C. E., p. 63). Satan took advantage of this blindness to cause some of their own educators, like wolves in sheeps' clothing, to prey on the lambs. Chief among these was John Sturm, who, by these blind reformers, was supposed to be a good Protestant. Sturm introduced practically the entire Papal system of education into the Protestant schools of Strasburg. And because he pretended to be a Protestant, the successors of Luther looked with favor upon his whole educational scheme. He was regarded by the so-called reformers as the greatest educator of his time, and his school became so popular among Protestants that it was taken as their model for the Protestant schools of Germany, and its influence extended *to England,* and thence *to America.*" "No one who is acquainted with the education given at our principal classical schools—Eton, Winchester and Westminster—forty years ago, can fail to see that their curriculum was formed in a great degree on Sturm's model." The historian says that it was Sturm's ambition "to reproduce Greece and Rome in the midst of modern Christian civilization." (Painter, p. 163).

THIS EDUCATIONAL WOLF, dressed in a Christian

fleece, made great inroads on the lambs of the flock, and made possible a Papal victory. Most dangerous of all enemies in a church is a school of its own, Christian in profession, "with teachers and managers who are only half converted; . . . who are accustomed to popular methods; . . . who concede some things and make half reforms, preferring to work according to their own ideas," (T. Vol. 6, p. 171), who, step by step, advance toward worldly education leading the innocent lambs with them. In the day of judgment it will be easier for that man who has been cold and an avowed enemy to a reform movement than for that one who professes to be a shepherd, but who has been a wolf in sheep's clothing, who deceives the lambs until they are unable to save themselves. It is the devil's master stroke for the overthrow of God's work in the world, and there is no influence harder to counteract. No other form of evil is so strongly denounced. "I know why works that thou are neither cold nor hot. I would that thou wert cold or hot. So then because thou art lukewarm and neither cold or hot, I will spue thee out of my mouth."

STURM'S SCHOOL stood as a half-way mark between the Christian schools of Luther and Melancthon and the Papal schools round about him. It offered a mixture of mediaeval, classical literature with a thin slice of Scripture, sandwiched in for effect, and flavored with the doctrines of the church. Its course of study was impractical; its methods of instruction mechanical; memory work was exalted; its government was arbitrary and empirical. "A dead knowledge of words took the place of a living knowledge of things. . . The pupils were obliged to learn, but they were not educated to see and hear, to think and prove, and were not led to a true independence and personal perfection. The teachers found their function in teaching the prescribed text, not in harmoniously developing the young human being according to the laws of nature." (Painter, p. 156). Macaulay, speaking of this system of education, adds: "They promised what was impracticable; they despised what was practicable. They filled the world with long words and long beards, and they left it as ignorant and as wicked as they found it." (M. B., p. 379).

JESUIT SCHOOLS.—This study should make it clear that the Protestant teachers weakened and unfitted the Protestant denomination for the attack made by th Papacy through the counter system of education introduced by Loyola, founder of the order of Jesuits Before this the Catholic church realized its helplessness to withstand the great movement of Protestantism, inaugurated by thousands of missionaries trained in the Christian schools of Luther and Melancthon. Noting the return of the Protestant church to dead orthodoxy under the inefficient leadership of Luther's successors, the Papacy recognized the vulnerable point in Protestantism.

THE ORDER OF JESUITS found its special mission in combating the Reformation. As the most effective means of arresting the progress of Protestantism, it aimed at controlling education. It developed an immense educational activity" in Protestant countries, "and earned for its schools a great reputation... *More than any other agency* it stayed the progress of the the Reformation, and it even succeeded in winning back territory already conquered by Protestantism.

. . . It worked chifly through its schools, of which it established and controlled large numbers. Every member of the order became a competent and practical teacher." (Painter, p. 166).

THE FOLLOWING METHODS of teaching are characteristic of Jesuit schools: "*The memory* was cultivated as a means of keeping down free activity of thought and clearness of judgment." In the place of self-government "their method of discipline was a system of mutual distrust, espionage and informing. *Implicit obedience* relieved the pupils from all responsibility as to the moral justification of their deeds." (Rosencranz, p. 270). "The Jesuits made much of *emulation*. He who knows how to excite emulation has found the most powerful auxiliary in his teaching. Nothing will be more honorable than to outstrip a fellow student, and nothing more dishonorable than to be outstripped. *Prizes* will be distributed to the best pupils with the greatest solemnity. . . It sought showy results with which to dazzle the world; a well-rounded development was nothing. . . The Jesuits did not aim at developing all the faculties of their pupils, but merely the receptive and reproductive faculties." When a student "could make a brilliant display from the resources of a well-stored memory, he had reached the highest points to which the Jesuits sought to lead him." *Originality and independence of mind, love of truth* for its own sake, the power of reflecting and forming correct judgments were not merely neglected, they *were suppressed* in the Jesuit system." (Painter, pp. 172-173). "The Jesuit system of education was remarkably successful, and for a century nearly all the foremost men of Christendom came from Jesuit schools." (Rosencranz, p. 272).

SUCCESS OF JESUIT SCHOOLS.—Concerning the success of the Jesuit educational system in overcoming the careless and indifferent Protestants, we read: "They carried their point." They shadowed the Protestant schools and, like a parasite, sucked from them their life. "Their labors were above all devoted to the Universities. Protestants called back their children from distant schools and put them under the care of the Jesuits. The Jesuits occupied the professors' chairs. . . They conquered the Germans on their own soil, in their very home, and wrested from them a part of their native land." (Von Ranke, Vol. 4, pp. 134-139).

This conquest rapidly went on through nearly all European countries. They conquered England by taking English youth to Rome and educating them in Jesuit schools, and sending them back as missionaries and teachers to their native land. And thus they were established in the schools of England. The Jesuits overran the new world also, becoming thoroughly established, and have been employing their characteristic methods here ever since. Here, as elsewhere, their only purpose is "to obtain the sole direction of education, so that by getting the young into their hands they can fashion them after their own pattern." (Footprints of the Jesuits, p. 419).

"Within fifty years from the day Luther burned the Bull of Leo before the gates of Wittenberg Protestantism gained its highest ascendency, an ascendency which it soon lost, and which it has never regained." (M. R.)

"How was it that Protestantism did so much, yet did no more? How was it that the church of Rome, having lost a large part of Europe, not only ceased to lose, but actually regained nearly half of what she had lost? This is certainly a most curious and important question." We have already had the answer, but it is well stated thus by Macaulay, who understood the part played by the Jesuit schools founded by Loyola: "Such was the celebrated Ignatus Loyola, who, in the great reaction, bore the same part which Luther bore in the great Protestant movement. It was at the feet of that Jesuit that the youth of the higher and middle classes were brought up from childhood to manhood, from the first rudiments to the courses of rhetoric and philosophy. . .The great order went forth conquering and to conquer. . . Their first object was to drive no person out of the pale of the church."

HERESY HUNTING DEFEATS THE PROTESTANT CAUSE: —Macaulay thus gives the causes for this defeat of Protestantism and the success of the Papacy: "The war between Luther and Leo was a war between firm faith and unbelief; between zeal and apathy; between energy and indolence; between seriousness and frivolity; between a pure morality and vice. Very different was the war which degenerate Protestantism had to wage against regenerate Catholicism," made possible by the Jesuit educational system. "The reformers had contracted some of the corruptions which had been justly censured in the Church of Rome. They had become lukewarm and worldly. Their great old leaders had been borne to the grave and had left no successors. . . Everywhere on the Protestant side we see langor; everywhere on the Catholic side we see ardor and devotion. Almost the whole zeal of the *Protestants* was directed against each other. Within the *Catholic church* there were no serious disputes on points of doctrine. . . On the other hand, the force which ought to have fought the battle of the Reformation was exhausted in civil conflict."

THE PAPACY LEARNED A BITTER LESSON IN DEALING WITH HERETICS. SINCE THE REFORMATION SHE CONSERVES HER STRENGTH BY SETTING THEM TO WORK. Macaulay says, "Rome thoroughly understands what no other church has ever understood—how to deal with enthusiasts. . . The Catholic church neither submits to enthusiasm nor prescribes it, *but uses it*. . . She accordingly enlists him (the enthusiast) in her services. . . ·For a man thus minded there is within the pale of the establishment (Orthodox Protestant churches) no place. He has been at no college; . . . and he is told that if he remains in the communion of the church he must do so as a hearer, and that, if he is resolved to be a teacher, he must begin by being a schismatic (a heretic). His choice is soon made; he harangues on Tower Hill or in Smithfield. A congregation is formed, and in a few weeks the (Protestant) church has lost forever a hundred families."

The Papacy was wiser than the Protestants in dealing with those who became somewhat irregular in their views. She spent little time in church trials. She directed their efforts, instead of attempting to force them from the church. "The ignorant enthusiast whom the English church makes . . . a most dangerous enemy, the Catholic church makes a champion. She bids him nurse his beard, covers him with a gown and hood of coarse dark stuff, ties a rope about his waist, and sends him forth to teach in her name. He costs her nothing. He takes not a ducat away from the regular clergy. He lives by the alms of those who respect his spiritual character and are grateful for his instructions. . . All this influence is employed to strengthen the church. . . In this way the church of Rome unites in herself all the strength of the establishment (organization) and all the strength of dissent. . . Place Ignatius Loyola at Oxford. He is certain to become the head of a formidable secession. Place John Wesley at Rome. He is certain to be the first general of a new society devoted to the interest and honor of the church." (M. R.)

The church of Rome since its rejuvenation is literally alive with determined, enthusiastic, zealous soldiers who know nothing but to live, to be spent, and to die for the church. She is determined to conquer and bring back humiliated, broken down, and completely subjugated, the Protestant denominations. She has everywhere, through her Jesuit teachers, editors, and public officials, men at work to fashion public sentiment, to capture the important and controlling positions of government and most of all, to obtain control through her teachers of the minds of Protestant children and youth. She values that eternal principle, and makes use of it, "Train up a child in the way he should go, and when he is old he will not depart from it." Let me teach a child until he is twelve years old, say the Catholics, and he will always remain a Catholic. We can now better comprehend why those English reformers did not understand the character and the danger of the school system in vogue at Cambridge, Oxford, Eton, and Westminster, and unwittingly planted this system of education upon the shores of their new home and in every one of their Christian schools. They ignorantly fostered it and scattered it, and their successors, like the successors of Luther and Melancthon, became so infected with the spirit of Rome that by 1844 the Protestant churches were morally like their mother.

In this we have been tracing the roots which bore the tree of education in the United States. While Harvard, the first school in New England, at first "was little more than a training school for ministers," and "the Bible was systematically studied," yet it is plain to any student of Harvard's course of study that, aside from Bible teaching, its curriculum was modeled after Eton, Rugby and other noted English schools which were all based on Sturm's system. Yale, William and Mary, and other institutions of the United States are modeled after this same system. *Behold Protestant America training her children in schools which were modeled after Sturm's Papal schools.*

THE SECRET OF THE REJECTION OF THE PROTESTANT DENOMINATIONS IN 1844 is contained in the educational history just given. We see that, while they clung to the forms of Protestantism, their educational system continually instilled into the student the life of the Papacy. This produced a form of Protestantism imbued with the Papal spirit. This spells Babylon. *Should not our students seriously question the character of the educational system they are under,* lest they find themselves in the company of those five foolish virgins who are rejected in the time of the loud cry just as the great Christian churches were rejected at the time of the midnight cry because they failed to understand the "true science of education?" "They did not come into the line of true education," and they rejected the message.

CERTAIN DIVINE IDEAS OF REFORM IN CIVIL GOVERNMENT were received from God by some men in this country during the days of the wounding of the Papacy. These men dared teach and practice these truths. They fostered true principles of civil government to such an extent that the third angel's message could be delivered under its shelter. But the Papal system of education, as operated by Protestant churches, was a constant menace to this civil reform, because the churches would not break away from the mediaeval classical course with the granting of degrees and honors—without which it is difficult for aristocracy and imperialism in either church or state to thrive. But in spite of the failure of the churches to break away from this system, the civil reformers repudiated all crowns, titles, and honors that would have perpetuated European aristocracy and imperialism. The churches, because they still clung to the Papal educational system, became responsible, not only for the spirit of the Papacy within themselves, but also for the return of imperialism now so plainly manifesting itself in our government, and especially noticeable in such tendencies toward centralization as the trusts, monopolies and unions.

The year 1844 was one of the most critical periods in the history of the church since the days of the apostles. Toward that year the hand of prophecy had been pointing for ages. All heaven was interested in what was about to happen. Angels worked with intense interest for those who claimed to be followers of the Christ to prepare them to accept the message then due to the world. But the history quoted above shows that the Protestant denominations clung to the system of education borrowed from the Papacy which wholly unfitted them either to receive or give the message. Consequently, it was impossible for them to train men to proclaim it.

The world was approaching the great day of atonement in the heavenly sanctuary, the year 1844. Prior to this date, history records a most remarkable Christian educational movement and religious awakening. The popular churches were rapidly approaching their crucial test. And God knew it was impossible for them to acceptably carry the closing message unless they should "come into the line of true education"—unless they had a clear understanding of "the true science of education." These words were applicable to them, "Now as never before we need to understand the true science of education. If we fail to understand this, we shall never have a place in the kingdom of God."

WHAT THE PROTESTANT CHURCHES FACED IN THE YEAR 1844. WE SEVENTH-DAY ADVENTISTS ARE FACING TODAY. We shall see how the Protestant denominations opposed the principles of Christian education and thus failed to train their young people to give the midnight cry. Seventh-day Adventist young people, thousands of whom are in the schools of the world, cannot afford to repeat this failure. The moral fall of the popular churches causing that mighty cry,

"Babylon is fallen, is fallen," would never have been given had they been true to the principles of Christian education. If individual Seventh-day Adventists approach the loud cry with the same experience that the Protestants approached the midnight cry, they likewise will be foolish virgins to whom the door is closed. The virgins in Christ's parable all had lamps, the doctrines; but they lacked a love of truth which lights up these doctrines. "The science of true education is the truth which is to be so deeply impressed on the soul that it cannot be obliterated by the error that everywhere abounds. The third angel's message is truth and light and power." (T. Vol. 6, p. 131). Is not Christian education, then, the light to the doctrines? Papal education fails to light up those lamps, for it is darkness.

Surely it is a serious time for our young Seventh-day Adventists—a time when every teacher in the land, when every student and prospctive mission worker in the church, should look the situation squarely in the face and should determine his attitude toward the principles of Christian education. For "before we can carry the message of present truth in all its fulness to other countries, we must first brean every yoke. We must come into the line of true education." "Now as never before we need to understand the true science of education. If we fail to understand this we shall never have a place in the kingdom of God." *We are dealing with a life and death question.*

HISTORY OF EDUCATIONAL REFORM PRIOR TO 1844.

We now approach the study of the educational reform carried on among the Protestant denominations in connection with the first angel's message prior to 1844. The following statement shows that there was need of a reform in education at that time.

"When the truth for these last days came to the world in the proclamation of the *first, second and third angel's messages,* we were shown that *in the education of our children a different order of things* must be brought in." (T. Vol. 6, p. 126).

It is impossible, in the limit of time, to study in detail all the experiences of the group of more than sixty schools advocating reform in education before 1844. With no attempt to exhaust the subject, the object will be to show that the light of Christian education shown with sufficient clearness in various schools of the United States to give the Protestant denominations an opportunity to gather up these principles as they were developing in the various schools, to incorporate them in their own church schools, "to com into the line of true education," and to train an army of missionaries to spread the message to the world at that time. For convenience, the various phases of Christian education will be considered as follows: The Place of the Bible in Education; Ancient and Modern Worldly Classics; Elective Courses of Study, Degrees, and Honors; Reforms in Diet, Location of Schools, and School Buildings; Training for Self-supporting Missionary Work and a Layman's Movement.

The attitude of the Seventh-day Adventist student toward these problems will measure his efficiency in the proclamation of the third angel's message.

HISTORIANS QUOTED:—The history of the educational reform movement prior to 1844 from which we quote, has been written, in most part, by men not in sympathy with the reforms made at that time. Many of these schools, after relinquishing their reforms, developed the popular system of education. The educators connected with these schools in their later history are no more proud of that period which covers these reform experiences than is the man who has once known Christ, and has followed Him in simplicity, and has later gone to the world. Such a man is apt to make light of his religious experience, and excuse himself for his former attitude toward reform.

So these historians, writing after the reform period, have often pictured the reform in an unfavorable or even in a ridiculous light. Had we access to the reformers themselves, doubtless the movement would appear in a still stronger light. Enough is given, even by the enemies of the movement, to satisfy the reader that the Spirit of God did stir the hearts of educational and church leaders on these great reforms, and under its guidance they attempted to practice them.

THE PLACE OF THE BIBLE IN EDUCATION.

Over this question, the relation the Word of God should sustain toward other subjects in the school curriculum, has been waged the war of educators for ages. The leader on each side in this controversy understands that his victory depends upon the position which the Bible holds in the school.

The story of this contest between the two forces over the position of God's Word in the education of the young may be read in the following Bible history: "The people served the Lord all the days of Joshua and all the days of the elders that outlived Joshua. . . *And there arose another generation* after them which knew not the Lord. . . and they forsook the Lord God . . . and followed other gods, the gods of the people that were round about them, and bowed themselves unto them. . . And the anger of the Lord was hot against Israel, and he delivered them into the hands of spoilers that spoiled them . . . so they could not any longer stand before their enemies . . . Nevertheless the Lord raised up judged that delivered them. . . And it came to pass when the judge was dead they returned and corrupted themselves in following other gods."

This is a condensed history of ancient Israel. When the Word of God held its proper place in home and school, Israel was prosperous, and worldly nations said of them, "Surely this great nation is a wise and understanding people." Then we read that they would "forget the things" of God, and fail to "teach their children" the Word. These untaught children "mingled among the heathen and learned their works, and served their idols, which were a snare unto them. . . Thus were they defiled with their own works, and went a whoring with *their own inventions.* . . And He gave them into the hands of the heathen; and they that hated them ruled over them. . . Many times did He deliver them."

The student of the Bible can read in this history

of ancient Israel a series of reforms which exalted the Word of God to its proper place in home and school. This was followed by carelessness in regard to Bible study and the practice of its principles in home and school. This meant that the ideas of worldly men took precedence of God's Word, resulting in such weakness that the very people whom Israel was so anxious to imitate despised them for their imitating, and regarded them with such disgust that they reduced Israel to abject slavery; and Israel lost the esteem of the world, in exchange for which she had neglected the Word of God. In the educational world she became the tail instead of the head. It has been a battle royal between Christ and Satan, Christ ever placing the wisdom of his Word before His people as "the principal thing," "a tree of life," while the god of this world holds us in bondage whenever the love of the truth dies out in our hearts. It has ever been his purpose to "spoil through philosophy and vain deceit after the tradition of men, after the rudiments of the world." And so the question at issue between Christ and Satan in the educational controversy, past, present, and future, has been concerning the place of the Bible in the minds and lives of teachers and students.

The history of modern Israel may be written in the same language as ancient Israel, substituting only modern terms and phases to impress more vividly the comparisons and the applications. The generation beguiled into preferring worldly literature to the Word of God has seldom been able to apply these lessons to itself, because "the god of this world hath blinded the minds of them which believe not."

"Above all other books, the Word of God must be our study, the great text book, the basis of all education; and our children are to be educated in the truths found therein, irrespective of previous habits and customs. In doing this, teachers and students will find the hidden treasure, the higher education. Bible rules are to be the guide of the daily life. . . A new purpose must be brought in and find place, and students must be aided in applying Bible principles in all they do. Whatever is crooked, whatever is twisted out of the right line is to be plainly pointed out and avoided, for it is iniquity not to be perpetuated." (T. Vol. 6, pp. 127, 131).

Students in our Christian schools should test every fact and statement offered by the Word of God. All information that does not stand the test should be rejected as chaff, for it is not oil for their lamps, and will only hinder in giving the loud cry. "A different order of things must be brought" into our schools, and "crooked and twisted things" must be straightened by Bible principles. Had this principle been followed prior to 1844 students would have been prepared to receive the midnight cry, and to carry the message to the ends of the earth.

THE BIBLE IN OBERLIN:—Oberlin College, established in Oberlin, Ohio, in the year 1833, had a most remarkable experience in the training of Christian workers. A historian of the institution writes, "The Scriptures both in the English version and in the original tongues were considered to possess the highest educational value, and as such, they should be studied first, last, and everywhere between. . . The Bible is fit to be and ought to be, at least upon a par with the classics, and should have a place in every scheme of education from the primary school to the university. . . Should not the theological students read the entire Bible in Hebrew and Greek? Oberlin decided to restore the Bible to its place as a permanent text book in the whole course. . . Christian education without the Bible! A monstrosity in the religious world, a stumbling block to unbelievers!" (Oberlin, pp. 233-235).

The following words sum up the conclusions of a large class of scholarly men of that time who were endeavoring to bring about a reform in education: "In the dark ages the classics were first despised, then over-exalted, and the Scriptures belittled. Now, again, we see the Bible is good for style and taste. . . The Bible is overlooked and neglected in education. Let the Bible have its place. *Matters like these are not to be decided by the customs of the schools which are yet replete with many a usage which has come from the age of Cardinal Bembo."* (Idem, p. 235).

An earnest effort was made by many educational reformers to place the Bible where it belonged in the schools. The power of God attended this effort. Had not teachers yielded to the pressure brought by leaders who were in sympathy with worldly education, the history of the popular churches would have been entirely different, and that of Seventh-day Adventists also.

OBERLIN ALLOWED THE BIBLE TO SLIP FROM ITS EXALTED POSITION, and, after a lapse of sixty years, from the following words we judge that the Bible has not yet reached the place it should occupy even with our own students: "The Bible has not been made a standard matter in their education, but books mixed with infidelity, and propagating unsound theories, have been placed before them." (T. E., p. 150).

ANCIENT AND MODERN WORLDLY CLASSICS.

Students in a worldly system of education are inspired by ideas from the heathen classics and other worldly authors, even as students of Christian education are inspired by the Bible. The classics, or humanities, may not always appear by name in the curriculum of some so-called Christian schools, yet, if the system is not animated by the spirit of the Bible, the result of the education will be seen in worldly characters.

"Uninspired authors are placed in the hands of children and youth in our schools as lesson books— books from which they are to be educated. They are kept before the youth, taking up their precious time in studying those things which they can never use. . . All unneccessary matter needs to be weeded from the course of study, and only such studies placed before the student as will be of real value to him." (T. E., pp. 151, 232).

THE CLASSICS IN OBERLIN:—Educational reformers prior to 1844 endeavored to follow the truth in the subjects they taught. Oberlin among others had this experience:—"*Heathen classics*—these two words stand for another of the burning questions of sixty years ago. . . The subject was under debate everywhere abroad." President Mahan, in 1835, "objected to the present plan in relation to Greek and Latin, especially the latter. It was better adapted, he said, to educate the heathen than Christians. We can discipline the mind with the Hebrew and Greek Scriptures, and these can purify the mind. This is the opinion of the best men and the best scholars. Let us have less classics and more natural science, more American law, and history, more of men and things. Give us truth, facts, practical and available knowledge."

The annual announcement of Oberlin, issued in 1834, contains this statement, "The collegiate department will afford as extensive instruction as other colleges, varying from some by substituting Hebrew and sacred classics for the most objectionable pagan authors." The reason assigned for substituting the scripture in the original for heathen authors was "that certain classical authors were so abominably unclean that it is nothing less than criminal to put them into the hands of our youth."

Sixty years after this, we Seventh-day Adventists received the following instruction on this subject, because our schools had not taken the positive stand on the classics and worldly authors that these educational reformers took prior to the midnight cry: "Shall pagan and infidel sentiments be presented to our students as valuable additions to their store of knowledge?" (Counsel to Teachers, p. 26).

The Board of Trustees asked the Faculty of Oberlin "to consider with much prayer and deliberation whether the time devoted to heathen classics ought not to be improved by the study of the Hebrew Scriptures and natural science." Three years later the same trustees asked, "Should not the theological students read the entire Bible in Hebrew and Greek?"

Two years later they voted, "That no student should be denied the approbation of the college at the end of his course by reason of any want of knowledge of heathen classics provided he sustains well an examination in other branches needed to prepare him for preaching Christ."

The movement to substitute the Scriptures for the heathen classics met with favor in many schools. In 1830 a lawyer of great eminence, a graduate of Yale, made a plea for "Sacred vs. Heathen Classics." The President of Amhurst, the President of Cooper Union, and Professor Stowe of Dartmouth College, "were in full sympathy with a desire to see relatively less honor bestowed on the literature of ancient Greece and Rome, and relatively more honor on the literature of ancient Palestine." (Oberlin, pp. 231-235).

These quotations show that a number of institutions of learning which today advocate the classics, at one time in their history favored the substitution of the Scriptures for the classics.

ELECTIVE COURSES OF STUDY AND DEGREES.

Worldly education compels students, regardless of their needs or future work, to follow a prescribed course of instruction. It deals with students en masse. Christian education recognizes individual needs, and works to perfect individual character. It permits students, in counsel with teachers, to select subjects according to their future needs. The Papacy cannot thrive unless it puts students through a prescribed course, "the grind," to destroy independence and individuality. Protestantism is the reverse.

"This long drawn out process, adding and adding

more time, more branches, is one of Satan's snares to keep laborers back. . . If we had a thousand years before us, such a depth of knowledge would be uncalled for, although it might be much more appropriate; but now our time is limited." (T. E., p. 106).

ELECTIVE COURSES:—Thomas Jefferson in his declaration of Principles for the University of Virginia in 1823, said, relative to the stereotype curriculum: "I am not fully informed of the practices at Harvard, but there is one from which we shall certainly vary, although it has been copied, I believe, by nearly every college and academy in the United States. That is the holding of students all to one prescribed course of reading, and disallowing exclusive application to those branches only which are to qualify them for the particular vocations to which they are destined. We shall, on the contrary, allow them uncontrolled choice in the lectures they shall choose to attend, and shall require elementary qualifications only, and sufficient age." Boone further says, "This policy has been in operation ever since. . . There is no curriculum of studies as in most institutions of like grade. . . This is 'the freedom of teaching;' and is the correlative of that equally fundamental freedom of learning which in this country has come to be known as 'the open system, or elective system.'" (Boone, pp. 190-191).

JEFFERSON'S PLAN for an elective course was a blow at one of the fundamental principles of the Papal system which gives the student no choice, and, of course, was opposed by those controlled by the Papal system. Boone says, "In 1814, after numerous defeats and constant opposition from William and

Mary College, *from Protestant churches,* and from most of the political leaders of the time, Mr. Jefferson and his friends sought to provide a university" which recognized the great principle of liberty in education.

RANDOLPH-MACON COLLEGE, a Methodist institution, founded about 1828, grasped the light of Christian education and made an effort to break away from the mediaeval system which exalted the classics. Randolph-Macon took this action concerning the old mediaeval courses: The "elective system was adopted. . . It is claimed that more thorough work can be done under this system than under the old curriculum system, but students are not allowed to choose for themselves without consultation with the faculty. Practically every student has a curriculum chosen for him, according to the course he wishes to pursue." Randolph-Macon had a hard time, and failed to carry out the reform. "It was a new movement, and it encountered prejudice or cold indifference on the part of the preachers and the people." Jefferson, p. 243).

HARVARD, that school which imbibed the Papal system of John Sturm from the English Cambridge, and which led all other American schools in the Papal plan of education, was among the first of the older schools to attempt to come into line with true education on this reform. It began about 1824. "The experience of Harvard, during the long transition from a uniform required curriculum to a regulated freedom in choice of studies, might be helpful to other institutions. . . There was adopted a course described as by far the broadest plan enacted up to that time." The students were given large latitude in their choice of studies. They were permitted "to elect from the following subjects. . . It was a large concession and had a permanent influence upon the course." (Boone, p. 196).

YALE, which so closely imitated Harvard in its early history, was materially effected by the reform in courses made by Harvard, and allowed students greater freedom in the choice of studies. "Even Yale, which has been generally and very properly regarded as the conservator of the principle of authority in college instruction, has granted large liberty in a quarter of a century. . . So numerous were the concessions that nearly one-half of the work of the last two years was left to be determined by each student himself. The juniors elected about 60 per cent. of their work and the seniors about 80 per cent. . . From the standpoint of the ancients or even of a scholar of the Revolutionary period, the change would seem to be ruinous; but *no one longer denies either the necessity or the wisdom of the elective principle.* To permit choice is dangerous; but not to permit it is more dangerous."

THE UNIVERSITY OF MICHIGAN, years ago, loosened up, and "students were allowed to pursue special courses, and secure at their departure, certificates of proficiency."

CORNELL UNIVERSITY also grasped the principle of Christian education on the subject of elective courses. "Liberty in the choice of studies is regarded as fundamental."

In many wide awake schools this question is being asked, "Shall a B. A. degree be given where the clas-

sics have been omitted? JOHNS HOPKINS says, Yes."
(Boone, pp. 197-198).

A prominent educator thus summarizes the virtues of the elective system: It encourages the early choice of one's life work; it develops individuality; it gives a chance for individual choice and guidance; it gives opportunity to teach what the student most needs; it best holds the interest of the student; it will early reveal the capacity of the student.

The old established courses were arbitrary, and were necessary to build up an educational trust suited to the needs of the Papacy. Without such courses it was difficult to adumbrate students, making them efficient tools in the hands of the leaders. No one should be allowed, according to their ideas of training, to exercise the right of choice, for fear he could not be directed as an obedient servant by the system when engaged in his life work. Individuality and personality, all independence and originality could be pretty well crushed by putting the students through the regular prescribed course of study. No man was allowed to teach, preach or do anything of importance without first finishing a course and receiving a degree.

So the Lord, in order to prepare workers for the midnight cry, inspired the reformers to attack the hard and fast course of study that had been inherited, practically without change from past centuries—a course that held the students' minds on the dim and musty past; that blinded them to the interesting and practical things of life and unfitted them to enter life capable of putting into practice the things learned in school. Such a training was absolutely useless to one preparing to give the midnight cry.

DEGREES:—Christians must hold before the world "That all men are created equal; that they are endowed by their Creator with certain unalienable rights; that among these are life, liberty, and pursuit of happiness." The Papacy opposes these truths, and has found its most effective tools in overcoming these unalienable rights to be her educational system with its courses and degrees. On the one hand these destroy freedom, independence, and originality of thought, while on the other hand they develop class distinction, aristocracy and imperialism.

The apostate apostolic church in order to keep her members submissive to her will in teaching, found it necessary to develop an educational trust. This educational monopoly became effective and complete when she adopted the pagan scheme of rigid courses leading to degrees. She gave the form to Christianity, and for the Spirit of God she substituted the pagan spirit. The combination of Christian form and pagan life produced the Papacy. Hartman, writing concerning the educational system of the apostate church, says, "The conferring of degrees was originated by a pope." (Religion or No Religion in Education, p. 43).

"Many who professed conversion still clung to the tenets of their pagan philosophy, and not only continued its study themselves, but urged it upon others as a means of extending their influence among the heathen." (G. C. p. 508). "As long as we sail with the current of the world, we need neither canvas nor oar. It is when we turn squarely about to stem the current that our labors begin, and Satan will bring every kind of theory to pervert the truth. The work will go hard." (T. Vol. 6, p. 129). "There is need of heart conversion among the teachers. A genuine change of thought and method of teaching is required to place them where they will have a living connection with a personal Saviour." (T. E. p. 29).

THOMAS JEFFERSON, the man who wrote that grand old document, The Declaration of Independence, which announced to the world our separation from the Papal form of government, and which enunciates the divine principle that all men are created free and equal, endeavored to develop an educational system in harmony with the reform position which the government had assumed. He saw the necessity of discarding rigid courses and degrees, and introduced the "elective system" as we have seen. "At first he attempted to drop the long established academic titles, save that of M. D. and to adopt the simple title of Graduate U. V., the name of the school or schools in which the student 'had been declared eminent,' being expressed in his 'certificate,' which was to be 'attested' by the particular professor." (Jefferson, p. 153). Professor Tappan, first president of the University of Michigan, followed Jefferson's plan. "Students were allowed to pursue special courses, and receive at their departure certificates of proficiency." (Boone, p .191).

That "first attempts to change old customs brought severe trials," (Mrs. E. G. White) was well illustrated in the experience of the founders in the

University of Virginia, for "in a few years the Board and Faculty were forced to give up the reform."

We have seen that the popular demand for the old established course and degrees was too strong for Jefferson to withstand. Later the spirit of God stirred the churches by setting up an agitation in the Oberlin school, giving them an opportunity to get away from that system so effective in maintaining the Papacy, and to prepare the people of God for the midnight cry. Of Oberlin College it is said, "The democratic feeling, the spirit of equality, the absence of classes and castes, based upon mere artificial distinctness is almost as marked in the institution as in the village." (Oberlin, p. 398). "There has been no positive action by trustees or faculty in opposition to such degrees, only traditional repugnance. Even the common degrees, in course, have been sometimes held in disrepute among the students. Half of the class of 1838, which numbered twenty, declined to receive the degree, and the President announced at the commencement that those who desired the degree could receive their diplomas at the college office." (Fairchild, p. 267).

The pressure of the church controlling Oberlin was so strong that the reformers were unable to break away from the old educational system. Who can tell how much weight this failure had in reducing the the Prostestant churches to the condition called "Babylon?"

EMULATION, HONORS AND PRIZES.

The granting of degrees, prizes, honors, etc., is borrowed from the Papal system of education.

"In our institutions of learning there was to be exerted an influence that would counteract the influence of the world, and give no encouragement to indulgence in appetite, in selfish gratification of the senses, in pride, ambition, love of dress and display, love of praise and flattery, and strife for high rewards and honors as a recompense for good scholarship. All this was to be discouraged in our schools. It would be impossible to avoid these things and yet send them to the public school." (Mrs. E. G. White, R. & H., Jan. 9, 1894).

Before 1844 God was endeavoring to do for all Prostestant denominations what he is now endeavoring to do for Seventh-day Adventists. The educational reform prior to the midnight cry proved a failure. But he who shares in the loud cry must succeed in the educational reform.

"Oberlin is somewhat peculiar in the matter of marks, prizes, honors and the like. During the thirties when Mr. Shipherd and his associates were laying the foundations, there was much earnest discussion abroad concerning the value and legitimacy of emulation. . . in student life. Many of the foremost educators held most strenuously that they are not needed to secure the best results, while in general tendencies it was on the whole positively harmful and vicious. In every way it was far better to appeal to pupils of all grades as well as to all others by addressing only their higher nature. Influenced largely by such convictions, it has always been that, though recitations and examinations are marked and a record is kept, this is not to establish a basis for grading or for distribution of honors, but only for private consultation by the teacher, a student, or other persons concerned. No announcement of standing is ever made." (Oberlin, p. 408).

UNIVERSITY OF NASHVILLE:—While Oberlin was struggling over the question of prizes, rewards, classics, etc., other institutions were battling with the same problem. Doctor Lindsley, founder of the University of Nashville, the predecessor of the well-known Peabody Institute, established in this period, said, "The giving of prizes as rewards for scholarship was discarded," and the founder testifies that "a much greater peace, harmony, contentment, order, industry, and moral decorum prevailed." (Tenn. p. 33).

HORACE MANN, the eminent teacher and writer, and the father of the public school system in the United States, heartily disapproved of the classic system of emulation. Mr. Mann says, "I hold and always have held it too unchristian to place two children in such relation to each other that if one wins the other must lose. So placed, what scholars gain in intellect, yes, and a thousand times more, they lose in virtue. . . You know my view of emulation. It may make bright scholars, but it makes rascally politicians and knavish merchants." (Mann, Vol. 1, p. 515).

Mr. Mann was opposing the Jesuit Papal practice, so necessary to the success of their system of education, which says, "Nothing will be held more honorable than to outstrip a fellow student and nothing more dishonorable than to be outstripped. Prizes will be distributed to the best pupils with the greatest possible solemnity." (Painter, p. 171).

REFORMS IN DIET.

"The true science of education" gives the student a knowledge of the laws governing his body, and a love for those laws. Every Christian school should give its students a knowledge of the proper diet, proper clothing, and should acquaint him with those phases of life that make a successful missionary. A wave of reform in the matters of diet, clothing, and other important health principles swept over the country, and many educational reformers endeavored to introduce these practical subjects into their schools. The spirit of God was preparing them for the crucial test in 1844.

"Among the studies selected for childhood, physiology should occupy the first place. . . It should be regarded as the basis of all educational effort." (Mrs. E. G. White in Health Reformer). "While the schools we have established have taken up the study of physiology, they have not taken hold with the decided energy they should. They have not practiced intelligently that which they have received in knowledge." (U. T., May 19, 1897). "The health should be as sacredly guarded as the character." (C. E., p. 184).

THE FOUNDERS OF OBERLIN, moved by the spirit of reform said, "That we may have time and health for the Lord's service, we will eat only plain and wholesome food, renouncing all bad habits, and especially the smoking and chewing of tobacco, unless it is necessary as a medicine, and deny ourselves all the strong and unnessary drinks, even tea and coffee, as far as practicable, and everything expen-

sive that is simply calculated to gratify appetite."
(Oberlin, p. 86).

In 1832, Mr. Sylvester Graham, the inventor of
graham flour, "began to call men to repent of the
sins of the table. According to this classical authority, vegetables and fruit should constitute the
substance of every meal, and should be eaten as
nearly as may be in their natural state. Bread should
be made of unbolted wheat flour (that being the
natural condition), though rye and Indian are allow-
able if unbolted, likewise rice and sago, if plainly
cooked. Good cream may be used instead of butter,
though milk and honey are somewhat better. Flesh
meat and fish in all forms had better be banished
from the table. No fat or gravies are to be tasted,
nor any liquid foods like soup and broth. Pastry is
an abomination, and cakes in which any fat or
butter has been used. Bread should be at least twelve
hours from the oven, and twenty-four hours are
better. And as for condiments, pepper, mustard, oil,
vinegar, etc., and stimulants like tea and coffee, they
are to be by all means eschewed as deadly foes to
health." (Oberlin, pp. 218-219).

Professors Shipherd and Finney of Oberlin both
confessed to being restored to health through the
Graham diet reform. "The Oberlin pulpit became
aggressively Grahamite. The boarding department
of the school was placed in charge of a disciple of
Graham. "Tea and coffee were not introduced into
the college boarding hall until 1842—possibly a little
later. . . Many of the families discarded tea and
coffee, and a few adopted the vegetarian diet." Concerning the vegetarian diet, we read, "For two or

three years longer the students were furnished at the hall with 'Graham fare.' They were not restricted to this. A table was still set for those who preferred a different diet." (Fairchild, p. 83).

DIET REFORM IN OTHER SCHOOLS:—Oberlin was not alone in these reforms. "In Williams College an association was formed in 1831 comprising the majority of the students with board based upon the principles of abstinence from tea and coffee, and the use only of food, the simplest in every respect." "The same reform was recorded in the history of Hudson College." In Lane Seminary "it was the wish of the students to dispense with tea, coffee, and all luxuries, and to live on the principles of Christian simplicity and economy." "In Danville, Ky., and Maryville College, Tennessee, it was the same, because we wish our ministers free from dyspepsia and liver complaint." Oberlin's historian writes that "the company was large that used neither flesh nor fish, neither butter nor milk, neither tea nor coffee." (Oberlin, pp. 222-223).

HORACE MANN said, "We must pay far more attention to the health of the students, not only by teaching the physiological laws of health, but by training students to an habitual obedience to them. Solomon does not say *teach* a child in the way he should go, but he says *train* him, which means that the child should be required to do the thing himself, and to repeat it again and again, and ten times again until it becomes a habit."

Mr. Mann says further, "As physical exercise enters so largely into the means of securing health, it is certain that no college can ever maintain a general condition of high health among its students unless they spend some hours every day in muscular effort. Hence the Faculty of Antioch College requires exercise of its students every day. . . We encourage manual labor in every practicable way, and if a liberal public or a liberal individual would give us land for agricultural or even for horticultural purposes, we promise them that the old injunction to till the ground and dress it shall not be forgotten."

One will look far for a writer with a clearer grasp of the health principles as taught by the Word of God. After describing the increase of disease in the world because of the departure of man from God's original plan, Mr. Mann says, "It comes solely because man will break heaven's laws; because for the sake of money or for pride, disease will marry disease; because when God commanded man *to work*—that is, to take some form of exercise—in the garden—that is, in the open air—men will not exercise, and will live in dwellings which add artificial poisons to natural ones, and then breathe the virulent compound." (Mann, Vol. 5, pp. 342, 415).

If health reform must be taught by Seventh-day Adventist ministers and teachers, and understood and practiced by all who will triumph in the loud cry, we are forced to conclude that the Lord was giving the Protestant churches, through their schools, this health reform light because it was as necessary for them to understand and practice it before the midnight cry as for us before the loud cry. We are forced also to conclude that their failure to live up to the light on health reform unfitted them to appreciate and accept other light. So it is extremely dangerous for students now to carelessly relate themselves to this reform.

THE PROPER LOCATION FOR SCHOOLS AND COUNTRY LIFE FOR STUDENTS.

The Papal system of education is typified by the word centralization; it exalts man, his ideas and his ways. In other words it is a study of the humanities, of the artificial rather than the natural. Such a scheme of education can best be worked out in connection with city life. Therefore, Papal schools and those schools patterned after the Papal model are usually located in towns and cities. On the contrary, Christian education means decentralization; it exalts God and His works; it is a return to God's way of doing. This system can best be developed in the country, on a farm where is to be gained an experience necessary to the carrying of the last message.

"God bids us establish schools away from the cities, where, without let or hindrance, we can carry on the work of education upon plans that are in harmony with the solemn message that is committed to us for the world. Such an education as this can best be worked out where there is land to cultivate. . . This usefulness learned on the school farm is the very education that is most essential for those who go out as missionaries to many foreign fields." (Madison School, pp. 28-29). "Some do not appreciate the value of agricultural work. These should not plan for our schools; for they will hold everything from advancing in right lines. In the past their influence has been a hindrance." (T., Vol. 6, p. 178).

CONCERNING THE SCHOOL GROUNDS it is said, "This land is not to be occupied with buildings, except to provide the facilities essential for the teachers and students of the school. This land about the school is to be reserved as the school farm. It is to become a living parable to the students. The students are not to regard the school land as a common thing. . . They are to plant it with ornamental and fruit trees and to cultivate garden produce. . . The school farm is to be regarded as a lesson book in nature. . . Bring all your energies into the development of the Lord's farm. . . The reasons which have led us in a few places to turn away from the cities, and locate our schools in the country, hold good with the schools in other places. . . Had the money which our larger schools have used in expensive buildings been invested in procuring land where students could receive a proper education, so large a number of students would not now be struggling under the weight of increasing debt, and the work of these institutions would be in a more prosperous condition. . . The students would have secured an all-round education which would have prepared them, not only for practical work in various trades, but for a place on the *Lord's farm in the earth made new.*" (T. Vol. 6, pp. 177, 181).

We have seen that God was endeavoring to arouse the popular churches to accept Christian education. This meant a reform in the location of their schools. A few years prior to 1844, many educational reformers were influenced to establish schools away from the city and on the farm.

THE METHODISTS as early as 1735 under the direc-

tion of the Wesleys and Whitefield attempted to carry
out God's idea of education in Georgia. They established a school ten miles from Savannah. The
historian states, "Mr. Habbersham had located the
five hundred acre grant." Wesley stated that this
school should be " a seat and nursery of sound learning and religious education."

THE UNIVERSITY OF VIRGINIA ON A FARM:—
When Thomas Jefferson was making plans for the
University of Virginia in a report made "to the
Speaker of the House of Delegates, it is stated that
they purchased 'at a distance of a mile from Charlottesville . . . two hundred acres of land, on which
was an elegible site for the college, high, dry, open,
furnished with good water, and nothing in its vicinity
which could threaten the health of the students.'"
(Jefferson, p. 69).

OBERLIN ON A FARM:—Mr. Shipherd, the founder
of Oberlin College, writes thus of his early plans,
"We are to establish schools of the first order, from
the infant school up to an academic school, which
shall afford a thorough education in English and useful languages, and if Providence favor it, at length
instruction in theology—I mean practical theology.
We are to connect work shops and the farm with the
institution." A tract of land was purchased in the
unbroken forests of Ohio, and 640 acres of this were
kept for school purposes. The soil was clay and wet,
and the tract "had been passed by for years as unde-
sirable for occupation." For this very reason the
purchase was severely criticized. It was made
because the faith of the founders enabled them to see
some things that even land experts overlooked. Let

Seventh-day Adventists read the similar experience of
the founders of the Avondale school, Cooranbong, Aus-
tralia. The founders of Oberlin "were guided by a wisdom higher than human, since a location, almost
forbidding in its physical aspects, and for years quite
difficult of access, was a condition indispensable to
the formation of the character and the performance
of the work to which Oberlin was clearly called."
(Oberlin, p. 82).

RICHMOND COLLEGE (Virginia) was founded by
the Baptists in 1832. They "bought Spring Farm,
a small tract some four miles northwest of the city,
and there on the Fourth of July, opened a manual
labor school, called the Virginia Baptist Seminary."
(Jefferson, p. 271).

EMORY AND HENRY COLLEGE, a Methodist institution, was established in Virginia in 1835. It was
to be "what was called, a manual labor college, an
institution of learning in which the pupils were to be
trained to labor as well as to think. This manual
labor feature was a very prominent one in the enterprise, as it was first brought before the public. . . A
farm containing six hundred acres of highly productive land was purchased and paid for out of the first
funds raised. It was at first intended that this farm
should be cultivated by student labor, for which a
compensation was to be allowed which would assist
in paying the student's expenses." (Jefferson, pp.
253-254).

It would be interesting to study this reform further for many other schools followed this light and
secured locations away from towns and cities. When

manual training is studied this phase of educational reform will be brought again to your attention.

SIMPLICITY IN BUILDINGS.

REFORM IN EDUCATION INCLUDES THE BUILDINGS in which an educational institution is housed. The spirit of centralization is a necessary feature of the Papacy, and associated with the Papal educational system of mediaeval Europe there is usually found a certain characteristic form of buildings—buildings of the monastic order, dark, dingy cloisters, with which are associated long prayers, counting of beads, chained Bibles, cowls, gowns, mortar boards, night vigils, long examinations, degrees, parchment rolls; memory work instead of reason; sight not faith; thought not action. Boone says, "Monkish education seeks by means of complete silence to place the soul in a state of immobility, which, through the want of all interchange of thought, at last sinks into entire apathy and antipathy toward all intellectual culture." Think of attempting to give this kind of education in the open, free country, or in buildings with open windows through which streams the bright sunshine of heaven, surrounded by singing birds, working teams, milch cows, growing grain, and the sound of hammer and saw. Such surroundings kill this system of education as surely as light kills germs.

"The mistakes that have been made in the erection of buildings in the past should be salutary admonitions to us in the future. . . Our ideas of building and furnishing our institutions are to be molded and fashioned by a true practical knowledge of what it means to walk humbly with God. Never should it be thought necessary to give an appearance of wealth. It is not large, expensive buildings; it is not rich furniture . . . that will give our work influence and success." (T. Vol. 7, pp. 92, 93).

THOMAS JEFFERSON in his scheme for giving a democratic education discarded the mediaeval dormitory system of Papal schools. "Instead of constructing a single and large edifice which might have exhausted their funds, and left nothing or too little for other essential expenses, they thought it better to erect a small and separate building for each professor with an apartment for his lectures, and others for their own accommodations, connecting these cottages, by a range of dormitories capable each of lodging two students only—a provision equally friendly to study as to morals and order." Of the students' cottages it is said, "They consisted of one story dormitories exhibiting a not unpleasant effect," and these buildings had their "garden grounds."

This certainly called for self-government. It placed teachers and students on the same level; it encouraged simplicity of life; it was economical, and appeals strongly to those who are limited in the amount of money they can spend in school buildings and equipments. But still other reasons are given for this cottage plan. Jefferson said, "The plan offered the further advantages of greater security against fire and infection, of extending the buildings in equal pace with the funds, and of adding to them indefinitely hereafter. . . Instead of one immense building, I favor having a small one for every professorship, arranged around a square to admit of extension, connected by a piazza so that they can go dry from one school to another. *This plan is preferable to a single great building for many reasons,* particularly on account of fire, health, economy, peace, and quiet." "Such a plan had been approved in the case of Albemarle College. " "Cabal also was thoroughly convinced of the soundness of the building policy of the university. Even the enemies of the institution acknowledged that Jefferson's course was wise."

An influential visitor "had been won over to the university by a mere visit of inspection which impressed him with the extent and splendor of the establishment. . . There was absolutely nothing in the neighborhood of Charlottesville to attract either professors or students. Jefferson was compelled, by the necessities of the situation, to create something visible and impressive which compelled admiration." Before the opening of the university, Jefferson wrote of ten distinct houses for the professors, "each with a garden," and "an hundred-and-nine dormitories sufficient each for two students."

Jefferson saw the effect of architecture on the plastic minds of students, and said, "My partiality for that division is not founded in views of education solely, but infinitely more as the means of a better administration of our government, and the eternal preservation of republican principles." (Jefferson, pp. 69-101).

OBERLIN'S FOUNDERS came into line with the truth in the matter of simple buildings. "To increase our means of service . . . we will observe plainness and durability in the construction of our houses, furniture, carriages, and all that appertains to us."

(Oberlin, p. 86). "There is a plain, neat, simple style of building which commends itself to every man's enlightened good sense, and still will not be highly esteemed by the world, neither is it an abomination in the sight of the Lord." (Fairchild, p. 359).

THE COTTAGE PLAN for housing students was followed by other schools also. Of Oglethorpe University, one of the leading Presbyterian institutions in the early history of Georgia, it is said, "There was a row of dormitories of one-story for the habitation of students. . . These were placed twelve feet apart and each one was divided into two rooms eighteen feet square." (Ga., p. 83). This was in 1837 when Presbyterians were wrestling with the "true science of education," and were settling the question whether they would help proclaim the last message to the world.

The object of the Christian school is to train young people to "endure hardness as good soldiers of Jesus Christ." Worldly governments, when training soldiers, avoided those conveniences and luxuries that tend to make the soldiers unwilling to endure the hardships of the battlefield. They are not quartered in up-to-date hotels. But often the buildings of a school are constructed and equipped for the convenience of those who teach, house and board the students, rather than for the training necessary to fit these young people to become soldiers to endure hardness. The uniform, the manners, and the polishing in general, of the young student soldier receive more attention than actual drill from many of the officers who have had more experience in dress parade than in lying in the trenches. Need we wonder why such a large per cent of the students, after long training, prefer to take up work in an institution with up-to-date conveniences where good food, clothes, and a salary are insured, rather than to pioneer an enter-prise where they are thrown largely on their own resources? To what extent are large, well-equipped schools responsible for this? In these last days schools that teach students to be content with simple food and clothing, and encourage the spirit of sacrifice, and give the ability to say, "From henceforth that land is my country which most needs my help," will be in greatest demand by those students who expect to triumph in the loud cry.

It was on this principle that Thomas Jefferson constructed simple school buildings in which to train a class of men to promote the principles of democracy in the United States. And practically every government in the world has been effected by these principles.

The average teacher, when thinking of a training school, conceives of large buildings, equipped with modern facilities and conveniences, calling for a large outlay of means. You students have had no such plant before you here. Your school would scarcely be recognized as an educational institution by one having the ordinary conception of a training school. This chapel, the small recitation rooms, the dining room, the shops, cottages, and other buildings grouped about the farm, provide the school facilities. Our facilities are, as a rule, more simple than many of you have in your own homes. What is the result? Scores of students from this plant have caught a vision, and have recognized the possibility of building up a school with limited means. As a result, over thirty little centers are providing education to hundreds of children outside the church, while if these same students had received their training in a school well equipped and expensive, no doubt the number of schools started would be considerably less.

Again, the average person when thinking of a sanitarium has before his mind one of our large institutions with every modern convenience. You have had before you a small sanitarium consisting of three frame, one-story cottages connected by covered porches, equipped so simply that they can be duplicated in almost any mission. You have seen this sanitarium filled with patients and a list of persons waiting admittance. Many have had their ideas revolutionized by this small sanitarium, and several health homes are coming into existence to be conducted on similar plans.

These two illustrations are cited to show that the effects of surrounding buildings and equipments on the minds of students are beyond calculation. The light was given to the Protestants before 1844 to guide them in the erection of buildings, equipment and furnishings; in diet, dress and surroundings, so that a great army might be able, in a simple manner to sweep the earth with that mighty message, the midnight cry.

MANUAL TRAINING AND THE PRACTICAL IN EDUCATION.

The times demand an education which will produce men and women capable of doing things. The Papal system divorces learning from doing and disqualifies men and women for giving the final warning to the world. God stirred every denomination, prior to 1844, to put practical Christian education within the reach of the young people.

"Had the system of education generations back been conducted upon altogether a different plan, the youth of this generation would not now be so depraved and worthless. . . There should have been in past generations provisions made for education upon a larger scale. In connection with the schools should have been agricultural and manufacturing establishments. There should have been teachers also of household labor. . . If schools had been established upon the plan we have mentioned, there would not now be so many unbalanced minds. I have been led to inquire, Must all that is valuable in our youth be sacrificed in order that they may obtain an education at the schools? If there had been agricultural and manufacturing establishments in connection with our schools, and competent teachers had been employed to educate the youth in the different branches of study and labor, devoting a portion of each day to mental improvement, and a portion of the day to physical labor, there would now be a more elevated class of youth to come upon the stage of action, to have influence in moulding society. The youth who would graduate at such institutions would many of them come forth with stability of character. They would have perseverance, fortitude, and courage to surmount obstacles, and principles that would not be swerved by wrong influence, however popular. There should have been experienced teachers to give lessons to young ladies in the cooking department.

Young girls should have been instructed to manufacture wearing apparel, to cut, to make, to mend garments, and thus become educated for the practical duties of life." (C. E., pp. 11, 18, 19).

JEFFERSON, as we might expect, caught a glimpse of this important phase of education, and made an attempt to put it into operation in the University of Virginia. "He proposed what he called a 'School of Technical Philosophy'. . . To such a school will come the mariner, carpenter, shipwright, pumpmaker, clockmaker, mechanist, optician, founder, cutler, . . . soapmaker, tanner, saltmaker, glassmaker, to learn as much as shall be necessary to pursue their art understandingly. . . In this school of technicology, Jefferson proposed to group the students in convenient classes for elementary and practical instruction by lectures, to be given in the evening, so as *to afford an opportunity for labor in the daytime.*" (Jefferson, p. 84). Jefferson is quoted as saying, "No nation will long survive the decay of its agriculture." (Pagan vs. Christian Education, p. 43).

"THE SOCIETY FOR PROMOTING MANUAL LABOR IN LITERARY INSTITUTIONS was formed in New York in 1831 with nearly a score of eminent names among its officers. . . A tremendous impulse was given to the movement by the publication in 1833 of Theodore D. Welds' famous pamphlet upon manual labor, under the auspices of the society. It contained the testimony of hundreds of noted men, all to the effect that this panacea without question was mighty to heal. . . His report, when published, produced one of the sensations of the time." (Oberlin, p. 230).

MANUAL LABOR IN OBERLIN:—Oberlin was among

the schools of this period that placed themselves in the hands of God to be used in giving a practical education to hundreds and thousands of youth who would later be called to do strenuous service for the Master. The historian of Oberlin states that about the time that school started, there was " a wide-spread intellectual quickening, including radical reforms in educational methods." Mr. Shipherd, one of the founders of Oberlin, desired to be in harmony with the divine plan of education, and said, "Hundreds of promising youth will doubtless be educated for God's service, or not educated, as we shall or shall not provide for them the means of complete education by their own industry and economy."

In the first annual report of Oberlin published in 1834, we read, "The manual labor department is considered indispensable to a complete education." The historian states, "Honest toil would be honored, the richest and poorest would meet daily on a common level, the health of all would be secured, a magic stimulus would be imparted to both minds and morals; but the best of all, and most certain of all, whoever of either sex would gain an education could easily pay his way with the labor of his own hands."

Oberlin's industrial department, the historian says, "is furnished with a steam engine which propels a saw mill, grist mill, shingle and lath saw, and turning lathe, to which other machinery will be added. One workshop is now erected and supplied with tools, and others are to be added." "Manual labor was among the most indispensable elements of the Oberlin idea. Nothing did more for Oberlin's establishment and enlargement. For half a generation multitudes of students were brought in from the whole land over, who otherwise would never have entered its halls; and much more, in all probability, would never have gained an education."

One of Oberlin's founders in 1833 wrote "that a female department would be established on the manual labor plan, including housekeeping, manufacture of wool, culture of silk, appropriate parts of gardening, particularly the raising of seeds for market, making clothes, etc."

In fact, the object of Oberlin, as published in its first catalog, "is said to be to give the most useful education at the least expense of health, time and money; to extend the benefit of such education to both sexes and to all classes of the community; . . . the thorough qualification of Christian teachers both for the pulpit and for schools; . . . the diffusion of useful science, sound morality, and pure religion among the growing multitudes of the Mississippi Valley, and to the destitute millions which overspread the world, through ministers and pious preachers."

Manual labor met with intense opposition, but in 1833, Mr. Shipherd wrote jubilantly, "The scholars study and work well. Five minutes after the manual labor bell strikes, the hammers and saws of the mechanical students wake all around us." After naming the advantages of manual training, he adds, "In a word, it meets the wants of man as a compound being, and prevents the common and amazing waste of money, time, health and life." (Oberlin, pp. 98, 100, 223, 225).

NUMEROUS MANUAL LABOR INSTITUTIONS:—"In all this Oberlin was not in the least original, but merely copied, with slight modifications, what was to be found in numerous institutions throughout the eastern, middle and western states. In 1830, *ten* could be named having manual labor attachments, while during the next decade *several scores* were added to the number. Maine Wesleyan was famous in its day and was among the earliest, while Bowdoin, Waterville, and Bangor Seminary possessed these advantages. In Dexter, Maine, not only all students, but teachers also were required to labor at least four hours each day. Massachusetts had at least *half a dozen*. . . New York was favored with *several*, Oneida Institute being prominent; and the Rochester Institute of Practical Education, in which students of ordinary mechanical skill while learning a trade can nearly pay their board, and it is calculated, when certain intended facilities are furnished, they will pay all their expenses. Pennsylvania, too, *was well supplied*. At LaFayette College, Easton, President Jenkins and the students performed the labor of erecting a two-story building. . . In the west where people were poorer and land was cheaper, manual labor was most popular. Hudson (Ohio) had shops and a farm, Marietta and Lane Seminary the same, with at least as many more. Michigan moved in the great matter while yet a territory, nor were Indiana, Illinois, Kentucky, or Tennessee, in the least degree backward in ministering to the muscle of the student class." (Oberlin, pp. 229-230).

"THE EDUCATIONAL SOCIETIES OF ALL THE LEADING DENOMINATIONS were active participants, whether Baptist, Congregational, Episcopal, Methodist, or Presbyterian, and *most of the leading educa-*

tors were full of enthusiasm and zeal. . . The Episcopalian secretary could exclaim: 'We almost envy our successors in the academic course when something of the vigor of the fathers shall be found in the intellectual laborers of the day, and the sallow tinge of dyspepsia shall cease to be the uniform testimonial of a life of study.'" (Idem). Dr. Lindsley, founder of the University of Nashville, now Peabody Institute, was an advocate of manual labor. He "would have attached to schools of all grades, farms and workshops. These farms and workshops would serve a three-fold purpose. They would furnish the needed exercise, they would be useful in teaching trades, and they would give poor boys an opportunity of making a living."

EMORY AND HENRY COLLEGE, in 1835, was "a manual labor college, an institute of learning in which the pupils were to be trained to labor as well as think. This manual labor feature was a very prominent one in the enterprise. . . This feature was made prominent in these incipient movements, for the institution was built up by a people engaged almost wholly in agriculture and the mechanic arts, a people among many of whom a prejudice existed against a learned and lazy race." (Jefferson, p. 253).

MANUAL TRAINING IN BAPTIST SCHOOLS:—"In 1830, a few devoted men met in the Second Baptist Church at five o'clock a. m. to devise and propose some plan for the improvement of young men who, in the judgment of the churches, were called to the work of the ministry. . . They organized the Virginia Baptist Educational Society, and for two years aided approved young men by placing them in private schools. . . In 1832, the Society bought Spring Farm. . . opened a manual labor school, called the Virginia Baptist Seminary. . . The number of students ran up to twenty-six, about two-thirds of them preparing for the ministry. . . To this purchase of nine acres, six more were added in 1836. . . The design in adding more was to give more scope for the manual labor feature of the school. This was strenuously insisted on by the authorities as giving to the needy opportunity for self-help and to all opportunity for exercise. But it proved unpopular with the students. . . And finally as we read in the report of 1841, this feature . . . has been virtually abandoned." (Jefferson, p. 271).

THE GEORGIA BAPTISTS in 1833 founded Mercer University, a school " which would unite agricultural labor with study, and be open for those only preparing for the ministry. The idea of founding a manual labor school where theory and practice should be taught, a scheme much in favor with Georgia Baptists, seems to have originated with Doctor Sherwood, who was the first to demonstrate its feasibility in the academy established by him near Etonton in Putnam County." (Ga. p. 61).

We might multiply historical data concerning manual training schools during this remarkable educational reform preceding 1844. The examples given are typical of the experiences of more than sixty manual training schools of this period. To Seventh-day Adventist educational reformers, these experiences are thrilling. What would have been the results had the men responsible for these earlier reforms stood stiffly for these principles instead of yielding to the pressure brought to bear upon them by the leading brethren of their respective denominations? This opposition was hard to meet, but the failure of the cause was really due to lack of courage and devotion to these principles, for where there is intense courage and love for God's work, opposition only strengthens the reformers. Adventists know that angels were busy everywhere encouraging these reforms. It is a startling fact that these schools relinquished their hold on the manual training reform just about the time that the midnight cry was due. Had they remained true, history would have made a different story. The history of Seventh-day Adventist educational work also would have been different.

Had Oberlin, for instance, remained true to her manual training idea, her missionary workers, going as they did to the mountaineers of the South and to the freedmen of the South, would have changed the whole complexion of Southern history. It would have placed the Southern states forty years ahead of the present. Booker T. Washington's work for negroes would have been established a quarter of a century before his time. But "because men could not comprehend the purpose of God in the plans laid before us for the education of workers, methods have been followed in some of our schools which have retarded rather than advanced the work of God. Years have passed into eternity with small results that might have shown the accomplishment of a great work." (Madison School, p. 29).

ADVANTAGES OF MANUAL LABOR:—"The students were divided into small companies of eight or ten each, and each company placed under the supervision of one of the older students. . . . It broke the monotony of ordinary student life; it promoted health and buoyancy of spirit; in the hours of field and forest labor, there was found not only relief from study but such a variety of incident, that the students of those days found more means of solid enjoyment than others have since. . . . All the students except day students boarded in a common hall, where by practicing economy and with the help of the farm, a variable surplus was realized each year which was applied in making improvements." (Jefferson, pp. 253-255).

MANUAL LABOR, as a part of the curriculum in those schools training ministers and missionary workers, is a part of that "science of true education" which God made known to some men and women prior to the year 1844. It was one of God's ways of training practical missionaries for mission fields of the world. In spite of the fact that practically every Protestant denomination had some experience in conducting manual training schools, these denominations as a whole opposed the idea, and their persistent opposition finally forced the schools that had led out in the reform to close their manual labor departments. The closing of the manual labor departments is a signal for a return to the educational system of mediaeval Europe. They began to train worldlings instead of Christians. Herein lay one of the greatest mistakes of the Protestant denominations prior to the year 1844. Here is one of the reasons why they were unprepared for the midnight cry and the first angel's message. Manual labor in connection with education was called by men in these manual training schools " a panacea mighty to heal." The training school for Christian workers which lost that "panacea" became spiritually sick, and ceased to advocate Christian educational reforms. It is called "a missionary impulse," which through manual labor, "made it possible for the very poorest boy or girl to secure an education and thus enlarge his fitness to perform the duties of life."

OBERLIN'S FRUIT:—God rewarded this school richly for its adherence to truth and for the product of its labors, in spite of the fact that it was finally compelled to yield. Of Oberlin it is said, "Though the very name was so feared and hated, yet there were friends sufficient to desire and solicit more teachers than were to be had. The quality of their work was found to be so excellent that it was wisdom to swallow much prejudice in order to secure the benefit of their instruction." "One year . . . no less than 530 teachers went out for the vocation. . . Who can measure the benefit bestowed by these great companies of earnest-hearted men and women who, for more than a generation, expended their energy upon the children and youth by the tens of thousands. . . Oberlin is the fruitful mother of colleges. Olivet College, Tabor College, Benzonia College, Berea College, Fisk University, Talladega College, Atlanta University, Straight University, Emerson Institute, Howard University, and other schools and enterprises absorbed for many years the missionary activity of Oberlin men and women." Their students entered such "foreign fields as Turkey in Europe and in Asia, India, Siam, South America, Hayti, and Burmah." (Oberlin, p. 321, Fairchild, p. 341).

Students can readily gather from this brief sketch

how extended might have been the influence of Oberlin had she remained true to her reform. The words addressed to Seventh-day Adventist educational reformers apply with equal force to the founders of Oberlin. "Reformers have been handicapped and some have ceased to urge reform. They seem unable to stem the current of doubt and criticism." (T. Vol. 6, p. 142).

OPPOSITION:—Students will be interested in a few statements showing the decline of these same institutions under the blighting atmosphere of suspicion, criticism, and opposition of the leaders. Oberlin withstood the opposition longer and more successfully than most other schools. The following extract gives the reader a picture of the doubt and criticism brought against Oberlin reforms by the leaders in the Presbyterian and Congregational churches. "Manual labor, for example, had many friends and admirers, but a large number looked askance at the idea. The student did not need, and could not afford, four hours per day for toil upon the farm or in the shop. Nor was the financial result likely to be of any considerable value, either to him or the institution to which he belonged." So said the critics. "Thus heads in New England and elsewhere began to shake." Again, "I have some doubts about a project lately started in this region and which makes no small demands on our regard as an enterprise of benevolence. I refer to Oberlin for which large funds have been received and are collecting. What need is there of another university or college in the woods of Ohio, surrounded by other institutions but a short distance off, still struggling for an existence? . . It

is said to have *manual labor,* but so has Hudson. . .
Why should students be importuned to leave the institution where they are to go to Oberlin?" (Oberlin,
pp. 243-247).

YIELDING TO OPPOSITION:—"After the beginning
of the forties, we hear little of manual labor. With
the general increase of wealth there was less need
of whatever pecuniary value it possessed. The con-
sciences of the good were less scrupulous about seeking exercise outside of useful labor, and the modern
gymnasium and athletics soon began to make all-suf-
ficient provision for the physical well-being of the
world." (Oberlin, p. 231). Note the year when this
decline occurred.

Mercer University, referred to above, had this
experience: "In 1844, the manual labor system
which had been on trial since the foundation of the
Institute in 1833, was abandoned, having proved
inefficacious. Several other attempts had been made
during the same decade to establish manual, labor
schools in different places which with one exception
had likewise failed." (Ga., p. 65).

Do Seventh-day Adventists grasp the significance
of this date? God cannot forever bear with unbelief,
half-hearted efforts , and cold, indifferent trifling with
divine principles. "If all who had labored unitedly
in the work in 1844 had received the third angel's
message and proclaimed it in the power of the Holy
Spirit, the Lord would have wrought mightily with
their efforts. A flood of light would have been shed
upon the world. Years ago the inhabitants of the
earth would have been warned, the closing work
completed, and Christ would have come for the

redemption of his people. It was not the will of God that Israel should wander forty years in the wilderness. He desired to lead them directly to the land of Canaan. . . In like manner it was not the will of God that the coming Christ should be so long delayed." (G. C., p. 458).

MANUAL LABOR DISPLACED BY ATHLETICS, SPORTS AND GAMES.

No school can successfully maintain manual labor studies in its curriculum on an equality with other studies unless the purpose of God for such a practical training is recognized by both teachers and students. And when the purpose is recognized, the love, interest and enthusiasm generated by an education to do useful things brings more enjoyment and keen pleasure to the student than such substitutes for manual labor as sports and games can ever bring.

"The physical exercise was marked out by the God of wisdom. Some hours each day should be devoted to useful education in lines of work that will help the student in learning the duties of practical life which are essential to all our youth. But this has been dropped out and amusements introduced which simply give exercise without being any special blessing in doing good. . . The time employed in physical exercise, which step leads on to excess, to intensity in the games, and the exercise of the faculties, ought to be used in Christ's lines, and the blessing of God will rest upon them in so doing. . . Diligent study is essential and dilligent hard work. Play is not essential. The influence has been growing among students in their devotion to amusement, to a fascinating, bewitching power, to the counteracting of the influence of the truth upon the human mind and character. . . What force of powers is put into your games of football and your other inventions after the way of the Gentiles—exercises that bless no one. . . I cannot find an instance in the life of Christ where he devoted time to play and amusement." (T. E. pp. 190-192).

It is easy to determine the system of education in operation in any training school. Students who enjoy games and sports more than useful labor have certainly chosen a system of education that will give them little help in preparing to enter the hard places of the world, or to prepare for the latter rain.

We have already noted that opposition to useful labor in Oberlin brought this change: "The modern gymnasium and athletics soon began to make all sufficient provision for the well-being of the student world." Gradually, "Oberlin introduced modern baseball, football, and athletics in general," (Oberlin, pp. 231, 407), but "the gymnasium made its way slowly at Oberlin, because it seemed to be inconsistent with the manual labor idea." (Fairchild, p. 262). All this is in harmony with the statement concerning gymnasiums: "They were brought in to supply the want of useful physical training, and have become popular with educational institutions." (C. E., p. 211).

Before the end, all training schools that are breaking from "the necks of their students worldly yokes," and are bringing their students "into the line of true education," so they may "carry the message of present truth in all its fullness to other countries," will see that all of these substitutes, such as football, base-ball, etc., are replaced by the genuine, useful arts and trades.

STUDENT SELF-GOVERNMENT AND CHRISTIAN DEMOCRACY.

INDIVIDUALITY, ORIGINALITY AND INDEPENDENCE of thought and action on the part of the student are in the end destroyed by the Papal system of education and other systems derived from it. This system is intended by its promoters to destroy these vital elements of character in order to make the individual a willing, blind, obedient servant to the mandates of men. The Papacy can not prosper except as it does destroy these most god-like faculties of man. Individuality, originality and independence of thought and action are developed by Christian education. This system is intended to develop minds capable of being guided by the Holy Spirit, even though that way may be at times diametrically opposed to the rulings of men. They learn to take their orders from the Captain of the Lord's army whose hand is among the wheels of the affairs of men to prevent confusion, anarchy, and disobedience to any organization which is based upon correct principles.

God was preparing a company who could be guided completely by His Spirit in the giving of the midnight cry. Only those trained to take the initiative, to be self-governing, would dare break away at the call of God from the errors and customs of Rome as found in the Prostestant churches.

"THE MIDNIGHT CRY was heralded by thousands of believers. Like a tidal wave the movement swept over

the land. . . Fanaticism disappeared before this proclamation like early frost before the rising sun. . .
All were of one heart and of one mind. . . It caused
a weaning of affection from the things of this world, a
healing of controversies and animosities, a confession
of wrongs. . . Angels were sent from heaven to
arouse those who had become discouraged, and to prepare them to receive the message. . . It was not the
most talented, but the most humble and devoted who
were first to hear and obey the call. Farmers left
their crops standing in the fields, merchants laid down
their tools, and with tears and rejoicing went out to
give the warning. Those who had formerly led in the
cause were among the last to join in this movement.
The churches in general closed their doors against
this message, and a large company of those who
received it withdrew their connection. . . There went
with it an impelling power that moved the soul."
(G. C. pp. 400-402).

It does not require deep thought to discover the
cause of the failure of the educational system of the
Protestant denominations to train men and women to
participate in the midnight cry. The whole scheme of
education of that era, aside from the reform movement which was largely broken down by the pressure
of the popular church leaders, was to make men conservative, fearful of leaving the well-trodden paths of
action, and of course "the churches in general closed
their doors against this message." Protestant teachers
and preachers, in harmony with the Papacy, had for
years bound the minds of students and church members, to creeds both in education and religion, until
their adherents were governed by tradition, prejudice,

bigotry, and fear of their leaders. They had lost their love and power for self-government. Consequently, God could not lead them by His spirit; their organization was rejected; they had morally fallen; the second angel called them Babylon.

On the other hand, a few devoted schools, educational reformers and ministers, had trained a small company to prize the privilege of being governed by the Spirit of God as revealed in His word. They had practiced what they had been taught in self-government, until they were willing to follow the guidance of the Spirit. This shows that true self-government does not mean do-as-you-please; it means that self shall be governed by the Word of God. While this company was cast out of the church organizations, while they left their crops, their tools, and former employments of all kinds to participate in what seemed to those who had not learned self-government to be a fanatical movement, yet from such a company sprang the wonderful Seventh-day Adventist church. And this church is called to set before the world a system of schools, institutions and organizations of self-governing Christians, such as this world has never before seen.

THE CHARACTER capable of carrying the midnight cry had to be developed in the Christian manual training schools, or in the school of the common walks of life. The leader of this movement, William Miller, "the farmer prophet," like Christ and John the Baptist, was educated in the latter. His biographer, a man well qualified to judge the value of the popular educational system of the churches, writes, "What now, would have been the effect of what is called a regular course of education? Would it have perverted him, as it has thousands? Or would it have made him instrumental of greater good in the cause of God? Would it have performed its appropriate work, that of disciplining, enlarging, and furnishing the mind, leaving unimpaired by the process its natural energies, its sense of dependence and accountability as to God? Or would it have placed him in the crowded ranks of those who are content to share in the honor of repeating the twaddle, true or false, which passes for truth in the school or sect which has made them what they are? We think it would have been difficult to pervert him; but where so many who have been regarded as highly promising have been marred by the operation, he would have been in great danger. He might have become externally a better subject for the artist; *but we doubt if he would have been a better subject to be used an an instrument of Providence.* There are those who survive the regular course uninjured; there are those who are benefitted by it, so far as to be raised to a level with people of ordinary capacity, which they never could attain without special aid. And there is a third class, who are a stereotype representation of what the course makes them; if they raise a fellowman out of the mire, they never get him nearer to heaven than the school where they were educated. Whatever might have been the result of any established course of education in the case of William Miller, such a course was beyond his reach; he was deprived of the benefit, *he has escaped the perversion.*" (Miller, pp. 15-16).

This is that William Miller, "the farmer prophet," who later brought the first angel's message to Oberlin.

The futility of depending upon men who have not been trained to self-government has been seen in the midnight cry experience. Every Seventh-day Adventist is approaching his final test, just as the Protestant churches approached theirs in 1844. Ours will come with the loud cry, the latter rain. Those who lack training for self-government, those not able to depend upon their own efforts for support, who are not making the Bible the basis of study, and physiology the basis of every educational effort; all who, in other words, "do not understand the true science of education" will have no part in the kingdom of God or in the loud cry.

CHARACTER NEEDED FOR THE LOUD CRY IS SIMILAR TO THAT OF THE MIDNIGHT CRY:—"The message of the third angel will be proclaimed. As the time comes for it to be given with the greatest power, the Lord will work through humble instruments, *leading* the minds of those who consecrate themselves to His service. The *laborers will be qualified rather by the unction of His Spirit than by the training of literary institutions.* Men of faith and of prayer will be constrained to go forth with holy zeal proclaiming the words which God gives them." (G. C., p. 606).

The Jesuit schools taught their students blind obedience. The student was not required to go to God for wisdom regarding his conduct. His teacher assumed that responsibility. True self-government, which may be defined as bringing one's conduct into harmony with God's principles as expressed in His Word, was absolutely neglected. The terrible effects of the Papal system of school discipline has been seen during the first angel's message. Those students who

blindly followed teachers rather than God's principles
were bound by customs, traditions, organizations and
leaders at a time when the Spirit of God was calling
them to follow the truth. As a preparation for the
loud cry, we are told, "The plan of the schools we shall
establish in these closing years of the work is to be
of an entirely different order from those we have
instituted." (Madison School, p. 28).

"THE OBJECT OF DISCIPLINE is the training of the
child for self-government. . . Having never learned
to govern himself, the youth recognizes no restraint
except the requirements of parents or teachers. This
removed, he knows not how to use his liberty, and
often gives himself to indulgence that proves his
ruin. . . Students should not be led to feel that they
cannot go out or come in without being watched. . .
Lead the youth to feel that they are trusted, and there
are few that will not seek to prove themselves worthy
of the trust. . . It is better to request than to com-
mand. The one thus addressed has an opportunity to
prove himself loyal to right principles. His obedience
is the result of choice rather than compulsion. The
rules governing the school room, should, so far as
possible, represent the voice of the school. . . Thus
he will feel a responsibility to see that the rules he
has helped to frame are obeyed. Rules should be few
and well considered; and *when once made they should
be enforced.* . . Those who desire to control others
must first control themselves." "Co-operation should
be the spirit of the school room, the law of its life."
"Let the older assist the younger; the strong the
weak. This will encourage self-respect and a desire
to be useful." (Ed. pp. 285-292).

JEFFERSON, THE FATHER OF DEMOCRACY, knowing that self-government was not taught in the schools of his day, and that democracy cannot exist in the State unless its principles are first taught and practiced in the school, introduced this principle into the University of Virginia. "It is very generally known that at the University of Virginia exists a remarkable system of student self-government, by which a high morale and a manly tone of self-reliance have been successfully maintained" Self-government is contrasted with what is called "professorial espionage." Self-government established a frank and kindly spirit of co-operation between master and pupil. It repressed all dishonorable practices of cheating in recitations and examinations, and promoted a spirit of independence and self-respect." (Jefferson, p. 94).

OBERLIN found it necessary, in the training of the right kind of missionaries, to develop a system of self-government. In Oberlin "the democratic feeling, the spirit of equality, the absence of classes and casts based upon mere artificial distinctions, is marked. . . The Faculty never sought to lord it over the students as being themselves superior, nor have they insisted upon a particular show of honors, reverence, or respect even. They played the role of elder brothers to their pupils. Titles were unknown, and students addressed their teachers as 'Brother Finney,' or 'Brother Mahan.'" "Self-rule was the ideal. The assembled youth were to learn how to use freedom by being left free. A public sentiment was to be the controlling force. . . Each individual has full liberty to make the most of himself, and stands for just what he is worth in heart or brain. Class yells and class colors have come in of late, and occasionally class hats, canes, and the like; at rare intervals, a class robe, but with the consensus of judgment and taste against any wide departure from the fashions of dress elsewhere in vogue in good society." (Oberlin, p. 399).

IN OBERLIN, "the regulations are few. No strict personal surveillance was ever undertaken. The student has been thrown greatly on his own responsibility, with the understanding that his continual enjoyment of the privileges of the school must depend upon his satisfactory deportment. . . No monitorial system has ever been adopted. Each young man reports weekly in writing to the professor in charge, his success or failure in attendance upon prescribed duties. The young women report to the lady principal." (Fairchild, pp. 263-265). This sounds very much like the following: "The youth must be impressed with the idea that they are trusted. . . If pupils receive the impression that they cannot go out or come in, sit at the table or be anywhere even in their rooms, except they are watched, a critical eye is upon them to criticize and report, it will have the influence to demoralize and pasttime will have no pleasure in it. This knowledge of a continual oversight is more than a parental guardianship, and far worse. . . This constant watchfulness is not natural, and produces evils that it is seeking to avoid." (C. E., p. 46).

HORACE MANN ON SELF-GOVERNMENT:—In those days when the Protestant denominations were settling their eternal destiny, when they were determining whether they would hear the world-wide judgment message, and themselves be prepared for the midnight cry, such men as Horace Mann wrote, "One of the highest and most valuable objects to which the influences of a school can be made conducive, consists in training our children to be self-governing."

Mr. Mann had the following experience in dealing with students. He gave the young men to understand "that he looked to them to be their own police." "When a tutor who had resided in a gentlemen's dormitory to keep order was exchanged for a lady teacher, Mr. Mann appealed to the senior class one day after chapel service to know if they were not sufficiently strong in moral force to take care of the building without such supervision. They rose to their feet simultaneously, accepted the trust joyfully and confidently, kept the promise well, and transmitted its spirit to their successors." Mr. Mann, however, was always on the alert to assist these self-governing students by a word of caution, or by forewarning them of impending trouble. "It was Mr. Mann's pride and delight ever after to walk through the gentlemen's hall at any hour of the day or night, and to take visitors with him to convince them that a true spirit of honor and fidelity could be evoked from the young" in matters of self-government. At one time he wrote, "Our domitory, nearly filled with male students, has no tutor or overseer. In study hours, it is a quiet as your house. We have no rowdyism, no gambling or card playing, and we have nearly succeeded in exorcising profanity and tobacco." (Mann, Vol. 1, 438, 515).

"Go to the ant, thou sluggard;
Consider her ways, and be wise;
Which having no guide, overseer, or ruler,
Provideth her meat in the summer,
And gathereth her food in the harvest."

TRAINING MISSIONARIES TO BE SELF-SUPPORTING— A LAYMEN'S MISSIONARY MOVEMENT.

It was the divine plan that the midnight cry and the third angel's message should be carried to every nation, kindred, tongue and people. God wanted an army trained to carry forth this practical religion to a world which had been educated away from the gospel order by the pagan and Papal systems of education.

We have seen that Christian education, as developed by the educational reformers in every Protestant denomination, made possible a mighty laymen's movement. We can understand how these self-supporting missionaries could quickly carry the message to the world. It was Satan's studied effort to thwart this self-supporting laymen's movement. He accomplished his desired results by exalting worldly literature to a place above the Bible; by consuming practically all the student's time in mental effort, and leading him to depreciate the practical in education; by leading to a gradual substitution of athletics, sports and games for manual labor. Satan is endeavoring to deceive the very elect, the remnant church.

The Protestant denominations could not "carry the message of present truth in all its fullness to other countries," because they did not "first break every yoke" of worldly education; they did not "come into the line of true education;" they did not educate to prepare a people to understand the message, and then give the message to the world." (Madison School, p. 28).

SELF-SUPPORTING STUDENTS AND TEACHERS:— prophets) sustained themselves by tilling the soil or prophets sustained themselves by tilling the soil or in some mechanical employment. . . Many of the religious teachers supported themselves by manual labor." (C. E., p. 61). "Schools are to be established away from the cities where the youth can learn to cultivate the soil and thus help to make themselves and the school self-supporting. . . Let means be gathered for the establishment of such schools." (T. Vol. 7, p. 232). "The presentation in our schools should not be as it has been in the past in introducing many things as essential that are only of minor importance." (U. T., Jan. 9, 1909). "Your school is to be an example of how Bible study, general education, physical education, and sanitatium work may be combined in many smaller schools that will be established in simplicity in many places." (U. T., Jan. 6, 1908). "We need schools that will be self-supporting, and this can be if teachers and students will be helpful, industrious, and economical. . . Sacrifices must be made on every hand." (U. T., Jan. 24, 1907).

WORK FOR THE SELF-SUPPORTING LAYMEN:—"The time is coming when God's people, because of persecution, will be scattered in many countries, and those who have received an all-round education will have great advantage wherever they are." (Appeal for the Madison School). The apostle Paul "illustrated in a practical way what might be done by consecrated laymen in many places. . . There is a large field open before the self-supporting gospel worker. . . From heaven he receives his commission and to heaven he looks for his recompense when the work intrusted to him is done." (Acts, pp. 355-356).

Many educational reformers prior to 1844 were impressed by the Spirit of God to give a practical education in order that their students might be free to carry the truth to any field to which God might call. These reformers saw that the educational system in vogue in the Protestant churches was totally inadequate to prepare a missionary to dare to carry an unpopular truth contrary to the will of the leaders in those denominations. "Professor Finney of Oberlin College said, 'We have had the facts before our minds, that in general, the Protestant churches of our country as such were either apathetic or hostile to nearly all the moral reforms of the age. . . The churches generally are becoming sadly degenerate. They have gone very far from the Lord, and He has withdrawn Himself from them.'" "The churches generally did not accept the warning. Their ministers . . . had failed to learn the truth either from the testimony of the prophets or from the signs of the times. . . The fact that the message was *to a great extent preached by laymen* was urged as an argument against it. . . Multitudes, trusting implicitly to their pastors, refused to listen to the warning." (G. C., pp. 376, 380).

HUNDREDS OF SELF-SUPPORTING. MISSIONARIES were sent out by this same President Finney of Oberlin who "laid down the somewhat ultra and startling dictum that nobody was fit to be a missionary who was not willing, with but an ear of corn in his pocket, to start for the Rocky Mountains." (Oberlin, p. 328). This was the spirit of faith and daring awakened in the hearts of students who were taught to make their way from the soil.

THE AMERICAN EDUCATIONAL SOCIETY was the educational department of the Congregational denomination, and its work was to superintend all the educational institutions of that denomination. Oberlin was established by godly men in the Congregational church who desired to make their school a means of training Congregational missionaries. "Some of the candidates for the ministry made application to that organization for financial help . . . which step the trustees refused to countenance, but afterward, though grudgingly and unhandsomely allowed. . . Oberlin entered into a prolonged tilt with the American Educational Society of which the provoking cause was contained in certain pet ideas of the founders, notably, *the one with regard to self-support* to be made easily possible through the sovereign virtues of manual labor."

OBERLIN'S EFFORT TO TRAIN SELF-SUPPORTING MISSIONARIES, was attacked by Hudson College, a Congregational school which attempted to injure the influence of Oberlin in the denomination. "Here was too good an opportunity for Hudson to miss." In January, 1837, came this unjust criticism from Hudson, "When Oberlin started it was said that students would support themselves, thus not needing help. It operated against the Educational Society, and many refused to contribute, so when Oberlin became convinced that its scheme was visionary, and sought aid for students, the Board asked them to say frankly that Oberlin was not self-supporting, in order to disabuse the public of that notion. This has not been done. . . We are sorry they do not say right out 'We are not self-supporting.' So now it seems that Oberlin students cannot earn any more than others and need as much help. Thus Oberlin manual labor is no better than it is elsewhere." (Oberlin, pp. 249-250).

Oberlin was not always a favorite with sister institutions, and "was made to appear as a troubler in Israel, an Ishmaelite. Lane and Hudson had a grievance. Here was a shameless trespasser, a poacher upon their preserves." (Oberlin, p. 150). This was felt because of the "wholesale exodus of students who had flocked to Mr. Shipherd's school." The faculties of Lane and Hudson felt that "in all things, while Oberlin was radical, they were conservative. Yes, and Oberlin was overrun with students." and this in spite of the fact that "Oberlin wrought with all her might to restore to the churches the purely democratic polity of New England. Therefore, by a multitude of the good, Oberlin was abhorred and cast out as vile." "Oberlin is said to be manual labor, but so is Hudson. It is said that the students come from the east, but why should they come away from the excellent, long-tried, richly endowed, and well officered institutions in the older states to get an education in a meager and poorly furnished institute in the wilds of Ohio? Why should students be importuned to leave institutions where they are to go to Oberlin, as I understand has been extensively the case in this region?" So said Oberlin's critics.

THE MANAGERS OF OBERLIN FELT KEENLY THESE THRUSTS from their own brethren who occupied leading positions. The accusations were not true. Oberlin was sending hundreds of self-supporting missionaries to the Indians, the mountaineers of the South, to the freedmen, and to other needy fields. It aroused President Mahan to reply, "We do not feel called upon to say or do anything. We do not much care whether the Society aids our students or not. If we want help we can get it." "Thus stigmatized and cast out, what could Oberlin and her friends do but organize an educational society of her own? . . . Oberlin was charged far and wide with the sin of schism, with being the foe to church union, with tugging with might and main to overthrow the ecclesiastical status quo. . . It was presently Oberlin's lot to be cast out as vile, and but for the existence of the association and other subordinate bodies affiliated with it, Oberlin's students would have been unable to secure either license or ordination."

In 1839, the Congregational church put this query in their church paper regarding Oberlin: "Shall young men go there expecting to get a thorough, classical, and theological education? Will such be received by the churches as pastors or missionaries? Is there any obligation to aid Oberlin as now constituted?"

In 1840, two Oberlin students "asked to be licensed, and their case was referred to a committee, which without the least questioning, simply asked if they believed in the doctrines taught at Oberlin and their way of doing things. Declining to answer such an inquiry, it was finally changed to this, 'Do you believe on the whole, that Oberlin is a good institution, or is it a curse to the world?' They then confessed that they thought it was good, and also believed the committee would think so too if they would spend a week there." The license was refused these Oberlin students. (Oberlin, pp. 251-255).

THE CONGREGATIONAL CONFERENCE then took this action toward Oberlin, "We deem it inexpedient for our churches to employ ministers known to cherish Oberlin ideas." In 1841, this question was raised by the Conference of Ohio, "Will baptism pass muster as valid if administered by an Oberlin man?" The question was referred to a committee which reported, "Oberlin ideas are exceedingly dangerous and corrupting, and these preachers should not be received by the churches as orthodox ministers, nor should their members be admitted to the communion." "In 1844, the General Conference of New York condemned the heresy and censured the Genessee Conference for winking at it. . . The American Board discharged two noble missionaries, Bradley and Casswell in Siam for the same reason. . . The Cleveland convention was held this year, but the conference with which the Oberlin church was connected was not invited to a share in its deliberations. Mr. Finney and President Mahan were present, but a motion that they be invited to sit as corresponding members was voted down, by a considerable majority as one delegate testifies. But much of the time was spent in denouncing Oberlin, and the chief object of the convention seemed to be to destroy its influence, and exclude it from the pale of orthodoxy.

AMERICAN MISSIONARY ASSOCIATION FORMED:— "When Oberlin men would go as missionaries to the Northwest, it became necessary to bring into being, the Western Evangelical Missionary Society to send and support them, and when they undertook work in behalf of the negroes whether in Ohio, Canada or the West Indies or Africa, other organizations were required, which, in 1846, were united in the American Missionary Association, which also for years, with its operations, covered the home as well as the foreign field. . . The evil feeling which was very prevalent and widely extended found frequent expression in language like this: A delegate in the Cleveland Convention said, 'The influence of Oberlin was worse than that of Roman Catholicism.' The President of the Michigan University publicly avowed the belief that 'Oberlin theology was almost devilish.' Still another brotther said, 'Brethren, I hate Oberlin almost as badly as I hate slavery, and you know I hate slavery as I hate the devil.' "

WHEN OBERLIN STUDENTS APPLIED TO THE AMERICAN EDUCATIONAL SOCIETY to be sent as missionaries to the Indians, the Society replied, "We cannot. You are good men, and we wish you well, but it will not do." At another time, "the Board instructed one of its missionaries to be careful how he associated with Oberlin men on terms of too great intimacy, lest they be poisoned by their influence." An Oberlin student had applied for a position as minister in a Congregational church. The examining board asked, " 'If installed, will you allow President Mahan or Professor Finney of Oberlin to preach in your pulpit?' And as he replied that he would, a half day was consumed in considering if they should proceed with the examination. When one spoke of the Oberlin brethren, another said, 'They are not brethren, they are aliens,' and almost the entire body was in sympathy with this statement." (Oberlin, pp. 249-265).

Oberlin was being baptized with fire. These experiences were taken, in the most part, in a kindly spirit. They attended to their own business, and sent out a constant stream of live, enthusiastic, successful, soul-saving missionaries. They were beginning to appreciate the truth of this wonderful statement concerning Christian education: "When we reach the standard that the Lord would have us reach, worldlings will regard Seventh-day Adventists as odd, singular, straight-laced extremists." (Mrs. E. G. White, R. & H., Jan. 9, 1894). "I want you to guard one point; do not be easily disturbed by what others may say. Know that you are right, and then go ahead. . . Do not be troubled by the opinions of those who talk for the sake of talking." (U. T., July 18, 1892). Remember that Mrs. E. G. White refers to Oberlin history when the institution was passing through these experiences by saying, "The churches generally are becoming sadly degenerate. They have gone very far from the Lord, and He has withdrawn Himself from them." (G. C., p. 377).

Had Oberlin yielded to the demands of the church; had she not endeavored to obey God even under difficulties, she would never have accomplished what she did. For it was in the face of these experiences that she succeeded in placing more missionaries among the freedmen than all other American colleges combined. The spirit of the Lord helped Oberlin teachers to recogize under the conditions of that time, the principle in the following statement: "It is not the Lord's will that the work in the South shall be confined to the set, regular lines. It has been found impossible to confine the work to these lines, and gain success. Workers daily filled with zeal and wisdom from on high must work as they are guided by the Lord, waiting not to receive their commission from men." (Selections from the Test., p. 62).

A MANUAL LABOR STUDENT OF OBERLIN BECOMES PRESIDENT:—The experience of Professor James H. Fairchild, who was connected with Oberlin for over sixty years, first as a student and then as a teacher, bears witness to the fact that Oberlin did make it possible for students to be self-supporting. Professor Fairchild writes, "A very obvious reason for choosing this institution was my financial limitations." Speaking of himself at seventeen, he says, "My parents could spare me from the farm, but could not furnish money even for tuition. Oberlin was a manual labor school, and my brother and myself, taking the first course together, were manual labor students. On our first arrival we were put in charge of the lath-sawing in the mill, four hours a day, five cents an hour. This provided for our expenses the first year. The next and following years we worked as carpenters and joiners on the college buildings and the homes in the colony. By such labor, re-enforced by the wages of teaching in vacation, we earned our way through the entire course, without any sense of want or weariness, or any hindrance to our studies, or to our general preparation for the work of life." (Oberlin, p. 290).

This young man was a theological student, and with others from his class went out among the churches as a self-supporting minister. This was the preparation he received which fitted him to occupy a place first as instructor in Oberlin, and later as President of the institution with which he spent his life.

SALARY:—The character of the teachers that give students an inspiration to self-supporting work is thus described in the person of an Oberlin professor: "His piety is more like the divine Teacher's than usual; he labors with his might to do good in school and out; his education, though not collegiate, is sufficiently extensive; *he is a manual labor man; he does not teach for money but to do good; he is deeply interested in the West.*" Concerning the wages of this man, a member of the Board wrote, "I advise that you offer him $400.00 with the use of a dwelling-house and a few acres of land, hay for his horse and two cows, and his wood." Of the founders of Oberlin it is said, "These unselfish and self-denying souls offered themselves to the institution without salary for five years." (Oberlin, p. 209). Oberlin was able to be self-supporting, partly because she reduced the size of her faculty by utilizing student teachers, and partly because the members of her faculty were willing to sacrifice in the matter of wages.

THE STUDENTS who sought an education in such an institution were as strongly characteristic as the teachers. Of Oberlin students it is said, "With their own muscle, they were working their way into the ministry. Most were of comparatively mature years, while some were past thirty. . . It was a noble class of young men, uncommonly strong, a little uncivilized, entirely radical, and terribly in earnest." (Oberlin, p. 132).

SELF-SUPPORTING MISSIONARIES:—These schools which were wrestling with the problems of true education, were all of them, training missionaries and evangelists. They held a definite object before their students, a life work which called for self-sacrifice and devotion. This in itself put zeal and life into the work of teachers and students. The world was approaching one of the most momentuous years in its history. The judgment message was due. Intensity was taking hold of men in every station of life. Students in these schools were alive to the great social questions of the day, and instead of spending their time and energy in the study of dead classics, and other impractical subjects which have little or no value in the training of Christian workers, they were dealing with live problems which called for activity as well as thought. For instance, Oberlin students were devoting themselves to mission work among the Indians. They were educating the colored people; they were sending workers into the mountain districts of the South, and even into the islands of the sea. "Every long vacation numbers of Oberlin students made their way to Southern Ohio wherever the poor colored were gathered, and lavished upon them sympathy and compassion, receiving only their bare living."

"In 1836, Hiram Wilson, a Lane student, proceeded to upper Canada to work among the twenty thousand freedmen who had fled from slavery to that place of refuge. They were in deepest poverty and ignorance. To the task of Christianizing and educating them, he devoted his whole life. At the end of two years fourteen teachers from Oberlin were assisting him. In 1840 no less than thirty-nine were teaching colored schools in Ohio, half of them young women, receiving their board only, and as many more in Canada." It was such experiences that prepared these young people to do a most efficient work for the freedmen.

MUCH OF THIS WORK WAS ON A SELF-SUPPORTING BASIS. "The great body of young men who went out from Oberlin to preach in the early days, went as home missionaries—with this exception, that they looked to no society to aid the churches in paying their salaries. It was not difficult to find needy churches to welcome them. . . Such was the prevalent ignorance and misapprehension in regard to Oberlin, that the most they could look for was the privilege of working in some needy field without molestation. Each man was obliged to find a place for himself, and slowly secure recognition. Under these conditions. Oberlin men found their work and waited for a brighter day."

MISSIONARIES TO CUBA:—In 1836 a student seeking a warm climate for health's sake, went to Cuba. "Being a skilled mechanic he found self-support easy, and while there conceived the idea of a mission to the blacks of Jamaica to be carried on independent of any outside assistance." One of the missions started in Cuba was named Oberlin. "For fifteen years the call for recruits continued, and was responded to, until in all, thirty-six had gone forward. For several years, these much enduring men and women, aside from the pittance which the ex-slaves could bestow, depended almost wholly upon the labor of their own hands. In addition, they built their own dwellings as well as chapels and school houses."

OBERLIN WAS TRAINING MEN TO PROCLAIM AN UNPOPULAR MESSAGE, and these experiences were a part of their training. "A year or two of self-denying and efficient labor with some needy church without aid, was the usual probation to a recognized ministerial standing. Theological students going out to preach found no missionary society to guide them to open doors, and to secure them compensation for the service. They went where preaching seemed to be needed, and often returned as empty handed as they went, except for the friendship and gratitude of those to whom they carried the work of the gospel." One today might wonder how they lived, but the writer goes on to say, "They were manual labor students and could make their way in Oberlin another year. The situation had its advantages. The Oberlin man secured a theological standing of its own—a birthright of liberty. This freedom may have come at a heavy price, but it was worth the having." (Oberlin, pp. 322-325).

This is an illustration of the great principle given us: "Culture on all points of practical life will make our youth useful after they leave school to go to foreign countries. They will not then have to depend upon the people to whom they go to cook and sew for them, or build their habitation. They will be much more influential if they show that they can educate the ignorant how to labor by the best methods and to produce the best results. . . A much smaller fund will be required to sustain such missionaries . . . and wherever they may go, all that they have gained in this line will give them standing room." (Christian Schools, p. 47).

OBERLIN HELPS STUDENTS FIND THEIR. LIFE WORK:—Oberlin "never stood so exclusively as did the old-fashioned colleges for a culture purely scholastic in its nature for book learning. More emphasis was laid upon the practical side. Knowledge was good through its uses. . . Oberlin has always been impressed by the fact that what the world most needs is character, men and women of genuine worth and power whose aims are unselfish and noble, who count service a delight." The teachers "were overflowing with stimulus to thought and enthusiasm. . . The superficial, the namby-pamby, has been held in contempt. . . The mightiest questions were daily brought up for discussion." (Oberlin, p. 400). Oberlin "was composed wholly of elect persons, who came on a mission, with a burden, a definite purpose. . . One of the early graduates used to tell how, as he bade the class goodbye when he had completed his course in an eastern academy, the principal commisserated them upon the fact that they had been born so late in history that all the really important tasks had been performed, so that nothing remained for them but the ignoble work of helping to keep the wheels of progress moving along in the old ruts! But, entering the little clearing in the forest (Oberlin) he soon discovered that the universal conviction there was that a multitude of mighty questions were yet calling for solution; that the world's redemption was only just fairly begun."

ALIVE TEACHERS ARE MORE IMPORTANT THAN EXPENSIVE EQUIPMENT TO INSPIRE STUDENTS. "Among Oberlin's leaders were men of remakable power who uttered their convictions in such a masterful fashion as to make them deeply felt far and wide. Moreover, these men were of an intensely practical make. Thought, investigation, opinion found their fitting goal only in volition and action. Their definition of Christianity was broad enough to include every matter connected with human welfare. Every year they arouse and inspired hundreds of most impressible minds and hearts." (Oberlin, p. 298). "Say not, 'We cannot afford to work in a sparsely settled field, and largely in a self-supporting way. . . God desires that every man shall stand in his lot and in his place and not feel as if the work was too hard." (Words of Encouragement to Self-supporting workers, pp. 10, 14).

OBERLIN'S INFLUENCE FELT:—The historian gives the effect of such training in the following words: "It would be hard to over-estimate the part in this work which was taken by Oberlin missionaries. Remember that they numbered hundreds at an early day, and soon exceeded thousands. . . They scattered westward, eastward, and even southward, always pushing, debating inquiring, agitating. It bubbled from their lips as naturally as their breath, and they could not refrain from it. . . Oberlin is peculiar among all the learned institutions of the land in having so large a constituency of temporary students inculcated with her spirit, but not having her diploma; the bone and sinew of the country wherever they are; active and influential in their modest spheres, and always ready to second the efforts and sustain the work of her more authoritative representatives whenever they appear. . . There is hardly a township west of the Alleghanies and north of the central line of Ohio, in which the influence of Oberlin men and Oberlin opinions cannot be specifically identified and traced. It was the propaganda of a school of thought and action having distinct characteristics." (Oberlin, pp. 314-315).

Perhaps there is no other one experience that better illustrates the great power of Oberlin people, and their daring in taking the initiative against popular opinion, than their attaitude toward the slavery question, and the freedmen. When we see the work done along this line, we can better appreciate the value of Oberlin's system of education along the lines of Bible study, the discarding of injurious literature, her indifference to school honors, her manual training, self-government and self-support. Without such training, it would have been difficult for Oberlin students to pursue the course they did on the slavery question. It brought them in conflict with the laws of the land, but the students obeyed the laws of God rather than the laws of men. The following statement was addressed by a civil judge to an Oberlin man who was on trial for assisting a slave to escape: "A man of your intelligence must know that *if the standard of right* is placed above and against the laws of the land, those who stand up for it are anything else than good citizens and good Christians. . . His conduct is as criminal as his example is dangerous." (Fairchild, p. 125).

DESIRE TO REFORM AROUSED BY CORRELATION:— The secret of the success of Oberlin teachers in arousing students to take a stand on this debated question, and put themselves where they became leaders in a practical movement to arouse the minds of the people to the terrible wickedness of slavery as an institution, lay in the fact that Oberlin did not conduct her class work and her lectures along the regular stereotype lines of the schools about them. On the contrary, Oberlin *on every occasion correlated* this subject with the daily work in the classroom. One of Oberlin's enemies understood this secret at the time, and wrote, "With arithmetic is taught the computation of the number of slaves and their value per head; with geography, territorial lines and those localities of slave territory supposed to be favorable to emancipation; with history, the chronicles of the peculiar institution; with ethics and philosophy, the higher law and resistance to federal enactments. Hence, the graduates of Oberlin are masters of art in abolitionism, and with the acquirement of their degrees are prepared to go a degree or two further if occasion requires. . . They imagine that they are doing God's service. There may be some excuse for them (the students) but there is none for their instructors. We doubt if there is for either. So long as Oberlin flourishes and educates 1250 students per annum, male and female abolitionists will continue to multiply." (Oberlin, p. 265).

It has always been God's plan as illustrated by the schools of the prophets, that the Christian school should be the nursery in which reformers are born and reared—reformers who would go forth from the school burning with practical zeal and enthusiasm to take their places as leaders in these reforms. He intends that the teachers shall be leaders in reform, and possessed of sufficient ingenuity and adaptability to make a vital connection between every lesson and reforms. It was this method that made Wittenberg the center of the 16th century Reformation.

FEAR TO ACCEPT AND ACT REFORMS A MARK OF PAPAL SYSTEM OF EDUCATION:—It has ever been the policy of the Papacy to sterilize the brains of teachers so that they cannot be impregnated with reform ideas. The Papal system of education makes them content to repeat set lessons to their students, as they themselves learned them in school, with no thought of making practical application. The students, in turn, go out to teach others the same rote they have learned, and thus the endless treadmill goes on, ever learning, but never getting anywhere.

Macaulay thus describes this system: "The ancient philosophy was a treadmill not a path. It was made up of revolving questions of controversies which were always beginning again. It was a contrivance for having much exertion and no progress... The human mind, accordingly, instead of marching, merely marked time. It took as much trouble as would have sufficed to carry it forward, and yet remained on the same spot. There was no accumulation of truth. . . There had been plenty of plowing, harrowing, reaping, threshing. But the garners contained only smut and stubble." (M. B., p. 380).

Any school which, like Oberlin, has power to

arouse its students to carry out a reform for which God is calling, must expect to meet with the same bitter opposition from those who are content with the mere form of Christian education without the power of the Spirit. These are wells without water; clouds without rain, words without ideas, lamps without oil.

OPPOSITION AROUSES INVESTIGATION LEADING TO FRIENDSHIP:—In the days when Thomas Jefferson was meeting with the keenest criticism because of the reforms in education which he advocated, he found friends for his reforms even in the more conservative schools. For instance, Professor George Ticknor, a member of the Harvard faculty, made a careful study of Jefferson's views of education. He surprised his friends by traveling six hundred miles by stage-coach and the slow conveyance of that period, and endured with patience the annoyance of bad roads and the discomfort of bad inns. What was he thinking of in such a long journey southward? He was going to see Jefferson's new university fairly opened, and of it he wrote, 'that he found the system more practical than he had feared; he found an experiment worth trying.'" (Jefferson, p. 129).

OBERLIN'S ATTENDANCE A MYSTERY:—We have seen the jealousy and critical attitude of many of the leaders toward Oberlin. It was difficult for Oberlin to bear the irritation that was so constantly kept up, but God looked with pleasure upon the manner with which Oberlin met this persecution. "For the most part, little pains have been taken to forge or wield weapons of defense. She had gone forward patiently and persistently, minding her own business and doing her own work in her own way, assured that full vindication would eventually come. For one thing, all along she had the comfort of knowing that devoted and admiring friends were not wanting, and could see that a phenomenal success at many points had been achieved. With students of both sexes, she was fairly flooded. This same surprising and unprecedented growth in spite of extreme poverty, in spite of some serious errors and blunders, in spite of hosts of foes whose united strength seemed overwhelming, constituted a mystery which the most sapient of her calumniators was unable to solve. One of these expressed the perplexing fact to Mr. Finney something like this: 'It has always been understood that no institution could prosper or achieve success without having the sympathy and cooperation of both churches and ministers. In your case the multitude of these have either stood aloof, or have been actively hostile; and yet you secure students, teachers, buildings, and endowments far beyond the most fortunate of your neighbors. We cannot understand it at all.'" (Oberlin, pp. 263).

"No educational institution can place itself in opposition to the errors and corruptions of this degenerate age without receiving threats and insults. But time will place such an institution upon an elevated platform having the assurance of God that they have acted right." (Mrs. E. G. White, G. C. Bulletin, 1901, p. 454).

SELECTING AND TRAINING TEACHERS.

Undoubtedly, more failures have come to educational reforms and to schools, through the inability of the founders to select teachers in sympathy with

Christian education, and who have the ability to teach the essential branches as directed by the angels who wait to co-operate in the teaching of every class, than through any other one weakness. Teachers have been employed in Christian schools "who could pass well in a worldly institution of learning," but who could not follow the divine pattern as revealed to the founders. For this reason, many schools, established by reformers, soon patterned after the popular schools.

"God has revealed to me that we are in positive danger of bringing into our educational work the customs and fashions that prevail in schools of the world." (Madison School, p. 28). "Let not managers, teachers or helpers, swing back in their old customary way of letting their influenre negative the very plan the Lord has presented as the best plan for the physical, mental and moral education of our youth. The Lord calls for steps in advance." (U. T., Dec. 27, 1901).

Oberlin was terribly pressed by her own brethren who were ignorant of the nature and value of the educational light God had so generously revealed to her. But severe as was the criticism and pressure from the outside, Oberlin might carry out God's plan in the preparation of an army of missionaries to give the midnight cry, *had not some of her teachers continued to cling to the principles and methods of worldly schools.* The germ that finally caused her to stagger in her course was planted in her vitals by members of her own faculty. One example of the many that might be given is sufficient to make this matter clear. "Professor J. P. Cowles never looked with favor upon such dietetic vagaries; he did not scruple to ridicule and otherwise oppose them, and as he himself states, furnished pepper boxes, and kept the tables supplied with pepper for months, although eventually the prudential committee took them away." The influence of this teacher with some others who were opposed to President Finney's position on pepper and other condiments, tea, coffee, flesh foods, etc., and who failed to realize this health reform as an entering wedge, is thus stated, "Under the pressure of this panic, they rushed with precipitous and confused haste back to their flesh pots; and here, under the exhilerating influence of fresh infusions of the Chinese shrub, the Mocha bean, with the riotous eating of swine's flesh, and drinking the broth of abominable things, they succeeded in arresting a necessary renovating work." (Oberlin, 422-424).

OPPOSITION FROM WITHOUT, TRYING; FROM WITHIN, SERIOUS:—The nagging, the sneers, and the falsehoods of those outside Oberlin's walls, who were out of sympathy with her reforms, were unpleasant and serious obstacles, but the opposition of certain teachers who were continually undermining the love and respect of students for health reform was fatal to progress in all reform. In yielding on health reform, Oberlin began to relinquish her reforms one by one until she was unable to meet the test in 1844. Thus Oberlin failed in the great mission to which she was called by the First Angel, because some of her teachers were not in sympathy with Christian education. On those reforms where the faculty agreed, Oberlin made a world-wide record.

JEFFERSON'S SCHOOL finally lost out in its reforms because he was unwise enough to select a number of members for the faculty of the University of Virginia from the universities of Europe. Wise as was Jefferson on many great questions, he was weak on this point, and it is said that "Washington demurred; he doubted the expediency of importing a body of foreign professors who would be inclined to bring from the European schools ideas at variance with the principles of democracy," which Jefferson wanted to make basic in his school. (Jefferson, p. 45).

It was for this same reason that the staunch Puritan reformers lost their hold on those principles that would have prepared their descendants for the midnight cry. They established a number of schools, such as Harvard and Yale, that for years were recognized as Bible schools, but they were under the influence of teachers who, as we have learned, brought to them the Papal principles of education from Oxford, Eton, and other European schools, and this finally destroyed the desire for reform. If there is one thing above another that Seventh-day Adventists have been cautioned about, it is this point. Wrecks of Christian education have been strewn all along the way, just because teachers have opposed reforms as did that Oberlin teacher who insisted on putting pepper boxes on the tables, and ridiculed health reform and its advocates. Is it possible that some Seventh-day Adventist teachers have used their pepper boxes, filled with the most pungent and caustic remarks against educational reforms?

"It is most difficult to adopt right principles of education after having been long accustomed to popular methods. The first attempt to change old customs brought severe trials upon those who desired to walk in the way which God had pointed out. Mistakes have been made, and great loss has been the result. There have been hindrances which have tended to keep us in common worldly lines, and to prevent us from grasping true educational principles. . . Some teachers and amnagers who are only half converted are stumbling blocks to others. They concede some things and make half reforms, but when greater knowledge comes, they refuse to advance, preferring to work according to their own ideas. . . Reformers have been handicapped, and some have ceased to urge reforms. They seem unable to stem the current of doubt and criticism. . . *We need now to begin over again.* Reforms must be entered into with heart and soul and will. Errors may be hoary with age; but age does not make error truth nor truth error." (T. Vol. 6, pp. 141-142).

THE SPIRIT OF THE REFORMER:—In the days when the schools of the prophets flourished, the man who had these schools in charge was called "father," and the students were known as "sons." In New Testament times, one of the greatest teachers, barring the Master himself, speaks lovingly of "Timothy, mine own son in the faith;" and "Titus, mine own son after the common faith;" and "My little children of whom I travail in birth." He emphasizes still further the difference between the real teacher and the hired instructor, saying, "For though you have ten thousand instructors in Christ Jesus, I have begotten thee through the gospel." It is this spirit of fatherhood on the part of the teacher that makes for success. Emerson has said, "An institution is the lengthened shadow of one man." That one man is the "father."

We have already seen that many of the failures of the educational reform are to be laid at the feet of timid, unbelieving, conservative teachers; wherever there has been real success, and fruit has been borne in an educational reform movement, you will find one or more teachers who have served as fathers or mothers to the enterprise. As a rule, we must recognize that a school which is obliged to have frequent change of teachers or management, will see few results in the way of steady, healthy, educational reform. Luther and Melancthon were the parents of Wittenberg, and so long as they remained, the institution was a power for reform throughout Europe.

JEFFERSON AS A FATHER:—When in his 83d year, Jefferson would ride eight or ten miles on horseback over a rough mountain road to the University of Virginia. "This shows the deep interest with which he watched over this *child of his old age,* and why he preferred the more endearing title of 'father' to that of founder." Mr. Jefferson carried out this fatherly feeling through the last years of his life, for he used to entertain the students at Sunday dinner in his own home. "They might be young and bashful, but he knew the county from which they came, the men with whom they were acquainted, and he gave himself to the student family so completely that they soon felt at home." (Jefferson, p. 216).

OBERLIN HAD FATHERS:—Oberlin could never have accomplished what it did had it lacked this parentage. The relation of the founders to the institution when it was conceived in their minds is expressed in these words as they rose from prayer, "Well, the child is born, and what shall its name be?"

(Oberlin, p. 81). Their love for this child was manifested in the same manner that a parent shows love for its offspring; they toiled, sacrificed, and suffered for years without thinking of remuneration.

Of Oberlin's faculty it is said, "Among them was the conviction which nothing could shake, that the faculty ought to go 'by faith' in the matter of salary; that is, should not insist upon any legal obligation to pay them any definite sum, but be content to receive whatever happened to be forthcoming from the treasury." The spirit of fatherhood on the part of Oberlin men is revealed in the following experience of one worker: He "was so much delighted with what he found of religious fervor and democratic simplicity, that not long after he cast in his lot with the colonists, bringing several thousand dollars taken from his own purse or gained by solicitation from his friends. Elected a trustee, he was abundant in financial labors." (Oberlin, p. 284). The spirit of fatherhood means not only to sacrifice on salary, but to utilize your money and to solicit help from friends.

Mr. Finney also bore this same relationship to the institution. Many tried to entice him to what they liked to call more important fields and better remuneration, but he remained as president of the school for over forty years. As Elijah called Elisha from the plow to a subordinate place in the school of the prophets, that he might be trained to become a father when Elijah should depart, so Finney called Fairchild, a young man who had worked his way through Oberlin. Fairchild was afterwards offered lucrative and popular positions, but he chose to remain with Oberlin as a subordinate to Doctor

Finney at four dollrs per week, and there received the training which put him at the head of the school when Finney was called away. Fairchild's connection with the school lasted over sixty years.

These men each had a vision. Their students had visions. The fathers and mothers of Oberlin loved their children, and their example was not lost upon the students; for they went everywhere with the same spirit to father some enterprise for the salvation of souls. They never hesitated because a field was considered hard. They were as loyal to a hard field as their teachers before them had been loyal to Oberlin. It led Oberlin students to say, *"Henceforth that land is my country that most needs my help."*

WALKING WITH GOD, BUT NOT WITH A PERFECT HEART:—Of certain kings of Judah it is written that they "did that which was right in the sight of the Lord but not with a perfect heart." God used ProfessorFinney and gave him a view of the spiritual condition of the popular churches. He knew what the results would be if they did not reform. "Professor Finney of Oberlin College said, 'The churches generally are becoming sadly degenerate. They have gone very far from the Lord, and He has withdrawn himself from them.'" (G. C., p. 377). Stewart, Shipherd, President Mahan, all founders of Oberlin, understood the situation as well as Professor Finney. They all recognized that the only sensible way to bring about a permanent reformation in the Protestant denominations was through a system of Christian education, for "the hope of the future missionary work lies with the young." These men fought a good fight. They were all re-

formers of the highest type.   They belong in the class
with William Miller, Fitch, Himes, and others.

OBERLIN HEARS THE FIRST ANGEL'S MESSAGE AS
PREACHED BY WILLIAM MILLER AND FITCH:—"William Miller, having long since discovered things most
marvelous in Daniel and the Revelation, proceeded
for half a generation to turn the world upside down
in preparation for the end of this dispensation, which
this farmer-prophet fixed for 1843." (Oberlin, p. 66).
"The Rev. Charles Fitch came to preach the doctrine
of the immediate second coming of Christ.   He was a
man of much personal magnetism, intensely in earnest, profoundly convinced of the truth of his message, and called, as he felt, to bring the better light
to the good people of Oberlin." (Fairchild, p. 86).

The founders were greatly stirred, as were many
of the students.   But we have already seen the weakness on the part of some Oberlin teachers toward pre-
liminary reforms.   We have seen the terribly bitter
spirit manifested by most of the denominational leaders.   These things almost crushed Oberlin's reforms
until she was unable to meet the higher demands
made up her by the midnight cry.   Oberlin College
was not perfect in her heart, but God rewarded the
institution for the loyalty she had shown, and she
became a powerful factor in certain reforms in the
world's history, although she failed to have a part in
that reform of all reforms, the third angel's message.
It is well for Seventh-day Adventists to remember
that these things happened to Oberlin as an example
for those upon whom the ends of the world are come.
Oberlin teachers did not "break every yoke" of
worldly education, but "placed on the necks of their

students worldly yokes instead of the yoke of Christ." To us it is said, "The plan of the schools we shall establish in these closing years of the work is to be of an entirely different order than those we have instituted," but Oberlin decided to follow the methods adopted in the older established schools. She yielded to pressure, and thus began that "clinging to old customs, and because of this, we are far behind, where we should be in the development" of God's work. Oberlin men, just before their test came, failed to comprehend the purpose of God in the plans laid before them for the education of their workers. "They adopted methods which retarded the work of God. Years have passed into eternity with small results that might have shown the accomplishment of a great work." Oberlin, by yielding to opposition, unfitted herself to carry the message of present truth in all its fulness to other countries "because she failed to break every educational yoke." She failed at the last to come "into the line of true education," and as a result she could not give the final message to the world.

SOME EDUCATIONAL EXPERIENCES
OF SEVENTH-DAY ADVENTISTS.

The condition of the Protestant denominations in 1844 is illustrated by the five foolish virgin. When the midnight cry was given in the spring of that year, most of the leaders of these denominations took their stand against it. During the days of preparation, they had failed "to understand the true science of education," and they were not ready when the climax came. Some of their own educational reformers had endeavored to prepare the denominations for this great event, but these educational men were opposed and repulsed by their church leaders. Therefore, the leaders of the church were not ready to accept the first angel's message. Had the Protestant denominations "come into the line of true education," they would have accepted the first angel's message. This would have united them into one body again. "The church would again have reached that blessed state of unity, faith and love which existed in apostolic days when the believers were of one heart and one soul." (G. C., p. 379).

The popular denominations had been called by the Lord to prepare the world for Christ's second coming. They refused to obey, and "about fifty thousand withdrew from the churches." (G. C., p. 376). From this number came a few stalwart, daring, faithful Christians who became the founders and leaders of the Seventh-day Adventist denomination. The most of these sturdy leaders "had little of the learning of the schools." They had received their education "in the school of Christ, and their humility and obedience made them great." (G. C., p. 456). They were self-made, and had no need to spend much time to unlearn the wisdom received from that system of education which caused the ruin of the Protestant denominations of 1844.

Elder James White, in his life of William Miller, expresses in the following words his estimate of that system of education which ruined the Protestants: "What now would have been the effect of what is called a regular course of education? . . Would it have performed its appropriate work, that of discipling, enlarging, and furnishing the mind, leaving unimpaired by the process its natural energies, self-dependence as to man, and its sense of dependence and accountability as to God? Or, would it have placed him in the crowded ranks of those who are content to share in the honor of repeating the twaddle, true or false, which passes for truth in the school or sect which has made them what they are?" (Miller, pp. 15, 16).

SEVENTH-DAY ADVENTISTS CALLED TO BE REFORMERS:—These brave Christian reformers were now facing a situation similar to that faced by the Christian refugees who fled from Europe to the shores of America for the sake of developing a new order of things. But "the English reformers, while denouncing the doctrines of Romanism, had retained many of its forms." (G. C., p. 289). The founders of the Seventh-day Adventist church had left apostate churches, and they, like the English reformers, were impressed with the condition of these churches, but, while denouncing the papal doctrines found in the apostate Protestant churches, they failed to see all the errors in those churches. The reformers of 1844 also met persecution, as did the English reformers before they came to this country. For of them it is said, "Many were persecuted by their unbelieving brethren." (G. C., p. 172).

During the first few years of Seventh-day Adventist church history, we find the founders searching the Bible for the great fundamental doctrines of the third angel's message, which revealed false doctrines and certain fallacies that had crept into the popular churches; in writing and publishing those doctrines to the world; and in developing a church organization. They did their work well.

BUT WHAT WAS BEING DONE FOR THE EDUCATION OF THE CHILDREN AND YOUTH during this constructive period? Many of them were attending those same schools that had heretofore trained men to repudiate the light of the first angel's message. Many of the reformers were disturbed over the situation. They began to realize that keeping the children in these school would, in time, lead these children to regard truth as did their teachers who were out of sympathy with the message.

Light came from God on the problem of education. Seventh-day Adventist parents were instructed to take their children out of the public schools, and to establish schools offering a Christian training. "When I was shown by the angel of God that an institution should be established for the education of our youth, I saw that it would be *one of the greatest means ordained of God for the salvation of souls.*" (C. E., p. 24). To establish schools seemed too great a task to the majority of our people at that time. It was like the conquest of Canaan to the children of Israel. Many children from Adventist homes were taken out of the worldly schools, but the church lacked faith to establish schools and to grasp the Lord's promise to provide Christian teachers. So, for a time, the children were left without any school advantages. Parents realized that something must be done, but as they had not faith to obey the word of God in this matter, they gradually returned the young people to the worldly schools. Thus began the wanderings of Seventh-day Adventists in the wilderness of worldly education. They failed to understand "the true science of education." The work was retarded, and "because of this we are far behind where we should be in the development of the third angel's message." This experience came about the year 1860; in the year 1901, forty years after, this word came, "It is the beginning of the educational reform."

The following instruction came during this wandering in the educational wilderness: "There should have been in the past generations provision made for education upon a larger scale. In connection with the schools should have been agricultural and manufacturing establishments. There should have been teachers also of household labor. There should have been a portion of the time each day devoted to labor, that the physical and mental might be equally exercised. If schools had been established on the plan we have mentioned, there would not now be so many unbalanced minds. . . Had the system of education generations back been conducted upon altogether a different plan, the youth of this generation would not now be so depraved and worthless." (C. E., pp. 18).

From the pages of the Review and Herald we gather that there was considerable agitation over educational matters until the founding of Battle Creek College in 1874. By this time many of the leaders began to understand more fully the results of the terrible mistake made by not following the instruction given in the fifties concerning education.

The need of schools was apparent. Brother A. Smith, writing for the Review and Herald (Vol. 40, No. 2) , said, "Any one at all acquainted with our common schools is aware that the influences of their associations is terrible upon the morals of our children. . . I do not know why young ladies could not qualify themselves by a course of study at Battle Creek to serve as teachers of select schools in our large churches." This contains a suggestion for church schools.

A CHURCH SCHOOL was established in Battle Creek about this time. The teacher, who was the prime mover in this enterprise, was an educational reformer, and if the reform that he advocated had been favorably received and intelligently practiced, Seventh-day Adventists would have come out of the educational wilderness long before they did. The ideas on education which this man held were similar to the reforms taught prior to 1844. God desired that when educational work did begin among Seventh-day Adventists it should be on a basis at least equal to the educational reform movement before 1844. God had sent Seventh-day Adventists an educator who had accepted the third angel's message, and who was ready to begin the educational work among us at the point where the educational reforms ceased before 1844. This reform work accepted, would have placed Seventh-day Adventist educational work in a position before the world corresponding to that held by Seventh-day Adventist sanitarium work. The first Seventh-day Adventist sanitarium came quickly into line with all of the advanced ideas taught and practiced before 1844. And if there is one thing above another that has distinguished Seventh-day Adventists before the world, it has been their health reform principles and sanitarium work. They had an equal chance in the educational world.

The following words show what a serious mistake was made when this educational reformer who had come among us was criticised and his reforms rejected: "The present age is one of show and surface work in education. Brother ———— possesses naturally a love for system and thoroughness, and these have become habits by lifelong training and discipline. He has been approved of God for this. His labors are of real worth because he will not allow students to be superficial. But in his very first efforts toward the establishment of church schools he encountered many obstacles. . . Some of the parents neglected to sustain the school, and their children did not respect the teacher because he wore poor clothing. . . The Lord approved of the general course of Brother ————, as *he was laying the foundation for the school which is now in operation.*" (T. No. 31, p. 86). This church school developed into Battle Creek College.

BATTLE CREEK COLLEGE SHOULD HAVE BEEN ES-

TABLISHED ON THE LAND:—The promoters of Battle
Creek College were instructed to establish the school
on a large tract of land where various industries might
be carried on and the school made a manual training
institution, and conducted according to educaional reform ideas.   The following statement, which appears
in the General Conference Bulletin, 1901, page 217,
was made by Elder Haskell regarding the founding of
Battle Creek College: "I remember the time when
the present site was selected for the location of the
College here in Battle Creek. . . Sister White, in
talking to the locating committee, said, 'Get the school
on some land outside of the thickly-settled city, where
the students can work on the land.' "   In the same
General Conference Bulletin, pages 115 and 116, is the
following statement from Mrs. E. G. White concerning
the location of Battle Creek College: "Some may be
stirred by the transfer of the school from Battle Creek,
but they need not be. *This move is in accordance
with God's design for the school before the institution
was established, but men could not see how this could
be done.   There were so many who said the school
must be in Battle Creek.   Now we say that it must be
somewhere else.*   The best thing that can be done is
to dispose of the school's buildings here as soon as
possible.   Begin at once to look for a place *where the
school can be conducted on right lines. . . Get an extensive tract of land, and here begin the work which
I entreated should be commenced before the school was
established here. . .*   Our schools should be located
away from the cities on a large tract of land so the
students will have opportunity to do manual work."
From the above we see that when Battle Creek Col-

lege was established there was not enough faith and courage to build up an educational institution among Adventists in the country on a farm as the educational reformers prior to 1844 located their schools. The cause of this inability to appreciate the system of education for which God was calling was due to the fact that the leading men of the denominaion had received their education in schools that had repudiated the reform ideas advocated before 1844. The importance of manual training and kindred reforms had not been impressed upon their minds as Oberlin during her reform experience had stamped those ideas into the minds of her students.

Then, too, Seventh-day Adventists, a number of years before the establishment of their first college, lacked the faith to obey God in establishing simple schools on the right plan for educating the children that should have been taken out of the public schools. Those Adventist children whose parents, for lack of faith, failed to take them from the public schools, were now among the leaders of the denomination. Their faith and courage in the educational reform were weak, and their eyes were as blind to the true science of Christian education as were the eyes of their parents who had failed to provide Christian schools for them. The idea is thus expressed, "If ministers and teachers could have a full sense of their responsibility, we should see a different state of things in the world today, but they are too narrow in their views and purposes. They do not realize the importance of their work or its results." (C. E., p. 24). And so, because of unbelief, the first college was established where God said it should not be, and in the place of the reform principles and methods of Christian education, there were introduced the principles, methods, ways, studies, and ideals of the colleges of the Protestant denominations round about them. Therefore, under these circumstances, in this institution, were to be trained the future missionaries for the denomination,—those missionaries who should avoid the mistakes in preparing for the loud cry that ensnared the young people of the Protestant denominations before 1844 when approaching the midnight cry.

RESULTS OF THE FAILURE:—Our first college soon began to bear an abundant crop of worldly educational fruit, and the Lord gives plainly his estimate of this fruit and the system that produced it, and some sound advice as to the best course to pursue. *"If worldly influence is to bear sway* in our school, then sell it out to worldlings and let them take entire control, and those who have invested their means in that institution will establish another school, to be conducted, *not upon the plan of the popular schools,* nor according to the desires of principal and teachers, *but upon the plan which God has specified.* . . Our college stands today in a position that God does not approve." (E. No. 31, p. 21).

A CHANCE FOR REFORM :—It is not our purpose to enter into the history of Battle Creek College. It did much good, but its location and the system first adopted made it difficult to carry out Christian educational reform. However, at different times, strong efforts were made to bring about reforms. The following statement tells concisely the entire history of Battle Creek College: "Our institutions of learning may swing into worldly conformity. Step by step they may advance to the world; but they are prisoners of hope, and God will correct and enlighten them and bring them back to their upright position of distinction from the world." (Mrs. E. G. White, R. & H., Jan. 9, 1894).

Battle Creek College in Battle Creek, like Israel of old, swung back and forth between God's plan and the world's system of education. But she was a "prisoner of hope," and, as already stated by Mrs. White in the General Conference Bulletin of 1901, God brought her back to her upright position. In other words, He put her on the land where He said she should be founded, and where she could carry out the principles of Christian education.

We have seen that God sent clear and positive instruction to guide Seventh-day Adventist leaders in the location and establishment of their first college. We have been told that this instruction was not wholly carried out. Their faith was not strong enough for them to attempt to carry out this and other most important and fundamental principles of Christian education, such principles as making the Bible the basis of all the subjects taught; the discarding of harmful literature; the eliminating of traditional courses and their degrees; the making of physiology the basis of every educational effort; manual training; agricultural work; reform in buildings, diet, etc.

SEVENTH-DAY ADVENTISTS CLING TO PAPAL EDUCATION:—Their failure in all these directions was due to the same experience that caused the English reformers to fail in laying a foundation for educational work that would have qualified an army of Christian missionaries to give the first angel's message. "The

English reformers, while renouncing the doctrines of Romanism, had retained many of its forms." (G. C., p. 289). We have learned that while the English reformers broke away from Papal doctrines to a large extent through ignorance of the results they did not hesitate to adopt bodily the Papal system of education. They thought that sandwiching in a little Bible, and flavoring their teaching with some religious instruction, constituted Christion education. They were mistaken. The long history of spiritual failures in this country was the fruit. As a result of this ignorance, the Protestant churches were led down to a condition where they very closely resembled the Papacy itself and were called Babylon. Our own Seventh-day Adventist leaders left these Protestant denominations as the English reformers left the European Papal churches. They broke away from the Papal doctrines held by the Protestant churches, just as did the English reformers. But, like those English reformers, *they carried with them, from the Protestant denominations, an educational system that was Papal in spirit.* The English reformers struggled for years to stem the current of apostasy. They failed to understand the philosophy of their declining religious experience. Nevertheless, the results came at last, dreadful but sure; they were morally ruined and cast aside because they had failed "to come into the line of true education." It was a beautiful prospect utterly destroyed by the wiles of the arch deceiver. It was made possible through ignorance of the principles of Christian education on the part of many great and good men.

In these last days Satan will, if possible, deceive

the very elect. Is there any reason why he should not use the same method which has proved so effectual in his hands through all the ages—in the overthrow of the Jewish church and the apostolic church; in neutralizing, through the Jesuits, the great sixteenth century Reformation; in thwarting the efforts of the English reformers who attempted to establish on the shores of America the church for its final struggle?

Let us again trace the present system of worldly education to its source. The educational plan of our first college was borrowed largely from the popular religious colleges of the Protestant denominations. These denominations received their educational light from the older educational institutions of this country such as Harvard and Yale; Harvard and Yale, as we have seen, borrowed theirs from Oxford and Cambridge; Oxford and Cambridge are daughters of Paris University; Paris University, presided over by the papists, was wholly Papal, and is the mother of European Universities; she borrowed her educational system from Pagan Rome; Pagan Rome 'gathered into its arms the elements of Grecian and oriental culture;" Grecian schools drew their wisdom and inspiration from Egypt. "The ancients looked upon Egypt as a school of wisdom. Greece sent thither her illustrious philosophers and lawgivers—Pythagoras and Plato, Lycurgus and Solon—to complete their studies. . . Hence even the Greeks in ancient times were accustomed to borrow their politics and their learning from the Egyptians." (Painter, pp. 32-34).

EGYPT, THEREFORE MUST BE RECOGNIZED AS THE SOURCE OF ALL WORLDLY WISDOM that is worth studying. This worldly system of education from Egypt

is certainly enduring, or it would not have come down
to us through these long ages. It is this very Egyptian spirit of philosophy that has made so-called classical literature so attracive to men of this world.
The wisdom of Egypt has been kept alive in the world
by students, who, while in school, have studied her
philosophy and have caught their inspiration from
the classics. Strange to say, the most potent factor
in keeping this Egyptian education alive has been the
Christian church itself. For various reasons, at different times, she has not only allowed but encouraged
her young people to study these writings. Again and
again the church has been deceived by this Egyptian
wisdom as Eve was deceived by the knowledge of good
and evil. Christians have clothed this subtle philosophy with a Christian garb (Do you recognize the
Papacy?) and scattered it broadcast.

THIS EGYPTIAN PHILOSOPHY RUINED EVERY CHURCH
up to 1844, and Seventh-day Adventists have been
told that "now as never before we need to understand
the true science of education. If we fail to understand this we shall never have a place in the kingdom
of God." It is against this Egyptian philosophy that
God warns us in the words just quoted. It is this
very philosophy, so subtle, that God has in mind when
He warns the church that "If possible 'he' (Satan)
shall deceive the very elect." We young Seventh-day
Adventists should study the man Moses, who,
"learned in all the wisdom of the Egyptians, a graduate from the highest educational institution of the
world, and recognized as an intellectual giant, forsook
all the things that Egyptian education made it possible
for him to enjoy, and entered God's training school in

the wilderness. "It was not the teachings of the schools of Egypt that enabled Moses to triumph over all his enemies, but an ever-abiding faith, an unflinching faith, a faith that did not fail under the most trying circumstances." (T. E., p. 120).

After spending forty years in forgetting his worldly education and obtaining the wisdom of God, Moses was qualified to stand at the head of the largest industrial school ever known. "What an industrial school was that in the wilderness!" (Ed., p. 37). It took the students in this school another forty years to break the yoke of Egypt's educational system and to understand "the true science of education" so that they might have a place in the land of Canaan.

CHRIST CALLS MEN AWAY FROM THE EGYPTIAN SYSTEM OF EDUCATION:—But the most important thing for us Seventh-day Adventist young people is to study the great Teacher of whom it is said, "Out of Egypt have I called my Son." So completely was the Son of God called out of Egypt that as a child He was never permitted to attend even the Jewish church schools because they were so saturated with Egyptian worldly education. Seventh-day Adventist children have an equal chance. Study the Master in the humble home school at Nazareth, in the shop and on the farm, on the hills and in the valleys. He grew in wisdom until, at the age of twelve, he astonished the leaders of the church with the fruit of Christian education. "Mark the features of Christ's work. . . Although His followers were fishermen, he did not advise them to go first into the schools of the Rabbis before entering upon the work" (T. E., p. 136). Why? Because the schools of the Rabbis were filled with

Greek and Egyptian philosophy which blinds the eyes to spiritual truth. It was to a teacher from one of these schools that Christ said, "Ye must be born again."

God pleads with us to establish schools for our children that they may obtain His wisdom and understanding even in their tender years. Seventh-day Adventist students should forever turn their backs on this system of worldly education—the wisdom of Egypt—that has wrecked the prospects of every Christian church up to the Seventh-day Adventist. And we, individually, are in danger of this same Egyptian wisdom. "I am filled with sadness when I think of our condition as a people. The Lord has not closed heaven to us, but our own course of continual backsliding has separated us from God. And yet the general opinion is that the church is flourishing, and that peace and spiritual prosperity are in all her borders. The church has turned back from following Christ her leader, and *is steadily retreating toward Egypt.*" (T. No. 31, p. 231).

Before 1844 the Spirit of God sent messages to the Protestant denominations telling them of their condition in language very similar to that just quoted. They failed to understand it, because, as we have seen, the Papal system of education, which they unwittingly introduced into their church schools, had put out their spiritual eyesight, and had deafened their ears to the word of God. They did not understand "the true science of education;" they did not "come into the line of true education;" and they were rejected.

The student of educational history knows the force

cf the statement, "The church is steadily retreating toward Egypt," for this Papal system of education has its roots in Egyptian learning and philosophy, away from which God forever called His ancient people. Realizing the results that have come to other Christian bodies, we might be discouraged as we see our first school patterned largely after the colleges of the popular churches, especially in view of the fact that "the customs and practices of the Battle Creek school go forth to all the churches, and the pulse heart-beats of that school are felt throughout the body of believers." (T. E., p. 185). But we have the good promise of our God, "Our institutions of learning may swing into worldly conformity, but they are prisoners of hope, and God will correct and enlighten them and bring them back to their upright position of distinction from the world. I am watching with intense interest, hoping to see our schools thoroughly imbued with the spirit of true and undefiled religion. When the students are thus imbued . . . they will see that there is a great work to be done, and the time they have given to amusements will be given up to doing earnest missionary work." (Mrs. E. G. White, R. & H., Jan. 9, 1894).

SEVENTH-DAY ADVENTISTS CALLED TO BE REFORMERS:—Every loyal Seventh-day Adventist, realizing the parentage of our educational institutions, and the hope extended to them, will endeavor to help bring to an upright position every school found out of harmony with the divine plan. Every method used in our schools should be subjected to the divine test. "To the law, and to the testimony; if they speak not according to this word it is because there is no light in them." Everything should be discarded that does not prove to be genuine. Instead of treating the situation lightly or indulging in reactionary criticism, as men have treated reforms of the past, especially those reforms of 1834-1844, let us study prayerfully, the following instruction: "We need now to begin over again. *Reforms must be entered into with heart and soul and will.* Errors may be hoary with age, but age does not make truth error nor error truth. Altogether too long have the old customs and habits been followed. The Lord would now have every idea that is false put away from teachers and students. . . That which the Lord has spoken concerning the instruction to be given in our schools is to be strictly regarded; for if there is not in some respects an education of an altogether different character from that which has been carried on in some of our schools, we need not have gone to the expense of purchasing land and erecting school buildings." (T., Vol., 6, p. 146).

BATTLE CREEK COLLEGE THE MODEL FOR OTHER SCHOOLS:—As Battle Creek College was the first school among us, her example was followed by practically every other school established by the denomination. They modeled their schools after her course of study; they imitated her methods of teaching; and to a large extent followed her plan of location and patterned their buildings after hers. "The customs and the practices of the Battle Creek school go forth to all the churches, and the pulse heart-beats of that school are felt throughout the body of believers." (T. E., p. 185). These facts should help us to better understand the statement made when it was decided to move Battle Creek College out of Battle Creek on to a a farm. "We are thankful that an interest is being shown in the work of establishing schools on a right foundation, as they should have been established years ago." (G. C. Bulletin, 1901, p. 455).

The second school established among Adventists was located at Healdsburg, California. An attempt was made by the promoters of this school to follow the Lord's instruction in the matter of location. While Healdsburg was not located in the city as was Battle Creek College, yet, like Lot, the founders begged to go into a little city. Healdsburg College was located on the edge of a small town. While they endeavored to establish the manual labor feature, their unfortunate location on a small piece of ground, the retaining of traditional courses and degrees, and the strong influence exerted by Battle Creek College, soon swung Healdsburg into worldly conformity. But the words of hope were spoken to her also: "Step by step they may advance to the world, but they are prisoners of hope, and God will correct and enlighten them and bring them back to their upright position of distinction from the world." Over a quarter of a century after her establishment, Healdsburg College was moved to a large tract of land near St. Helena, California, and the college in its new location was in a position to begin its educational reform, as Battle Creek College is said to have come to its upright position when re-established on the land.

In Volume 6 of the Testimonies, page 139, our people are told, "Schools should be established, not such elaborate schools as those at Battle Creek and College View, but more simple schools with more humble buildings and with teachers who will adopt the same plans that were followed in the schools of the prophets."

Again, in the same volume we are told, "We need now to begin over again. Reforms must be entered into with heart and soul and will." (p. 142). We have seen the necessity for Battle Creek College and Healdsburg College to begin their work over again. The teachers in these schools now have a chance to "adopt the same plans which were folowed in the schools of the prophets," and to enter the educational reforms "with heart and soul and will."

TRADITIONAL COURSES:—One of the leading reforms called for in the Papal system of education deals with the question of courses and their degrees, because the moral fall of the Protestant churches can be attributed almost directly to the traditional courses offered in their schools and the attendant degrees. As a rule, their ministers were obliged to finish a course and obtain a degree, and this often affected their independence in following God's word; it checked their individuality and their originality. The school men are said to be "a stereotype representation of what the course makes them; if they (the graduates) raise a fellowman out of the mire, they never get him nearer to heaven than the school where they were educated. . . They are content to share in the honor of repeating the twaddle, true or false, which passes for truth, in the school or sect which has made them what they are." (Miller, p. 16).

THE PRIMITIVE CHRISTIANS carried the gospel rapidly and effectively to the world. In their school they taught only those subjects that would prepare the student to do the Lord's work. B y the world their educators were regarded as "odd, singular, straight-laced extremists." Everything was done by these Christian educators to prepare the student quickly to act the part of a good soldier in the battle. Students were not detained in the school to finish a course or take a degree, a custom in vogue in the worldly schools. Later, half converted pagan-Christian teachers introduced the course-and-degree idea which developed an educational trust controlled by the church leaders, and no one was allowed to teach or preach until he had finished a course and received a degree.

ONE OF THE MOST SERIOUS OBJECTIONS brought against this plan is that it closes the mind of the student to truth. Practically every religious reform has come through humble laymen because the church leaders, as a rule, in obtaining their education, have become conservative. Conservatism is the result of passing through a rigid, mechanical course of study for a degree. The student is held in a rut, on a treadmill; he is described as ever going and never getting anywhere. Consequently when the truth is presented to these school men, especially if it is brought by a layman, it is not looked upon with favor, as they have come to regard themselves as the regular channel through which light must come to the people. The truth of this statement is borne out by historical facts. Motley, giving the experience of reformers in Holland, writes thus of the restriction placed on laymen by the Papal system of education: "We forbid all lay persons to converse or dispute concerning the Holy Scriptures, openly or secretly, especially on any doubtful or difficult matters, or to read, teach, or expound the Scriptures, unless they have duly studied theology and have been approved by some renowned university." He adds, however, that "to the ineffable disgust of the conservatives in church and state here were men with little education, utterly devoid of Hebrew, of lowly station,—hatters, curriers, tanners, dyers and the like,—who began to preach; remembering unreasonably, perhaps, that the early disciples selected by the Founder of Christianity had not all been Doctors of Theology with diplomas from renowned universities." (Motley, pp. 261, 533).

The Lord sees that the rigid course with the degree often brings into the church "many men after the flesh. . . many mighty . . . many noble," instead of making leaders who realize that "God hath chosen the foolish things of the world to confound the wise . . . that no flesh should glory in his presence."

The most of the school men about 1844 rejected the first angel's message because it did not come to them in the regular way. "The fact that the message was, to a great extent, preached by laymen, was urged as an argument against it. . . . Multitudes, trusting implicitly in their pastors, refused to listen to the warning." (G. C., p. 380).

SEVENTH-DAY ADVENTISTS WILL BE TRIED ON THIS SAME POINT—"As the time comes for it (the third angel's message) to be given with greatest power, the Lord will work through humble instruments, leading the minds of those who consecrate themselves to service. *The laborers will be qualified rather by the unction of the Spirit than by the training of literary institutions."* (G. C., p. 606).

Satan will work with all his power of deception to have a company of men at the head of the Seventh-day Adventist church at the time of the loud cry who will regard the work of humble instruments led by the Spirit of God, who have not graduated from a literary institution, with the same disfavor as the leaders of the Protestant churches before 1844 regarded such irregularities. God wants thousands of men trained in our schools, but He does not want them to receive such a training that their attitude toward truth will be the same as that of the school men of other denominations prior to 1844. The question of most vital importance to us Seventh-day Adventists is, can we obtain a liberal, practical education for God's work without being spoiled in the training? There must be some way out.

WHEN BATTLE CREEK COLLEGE WAS ENCOURAGING STUDENTS TO TAKE COURSES leading to degrees modeled after the worldly schools, it received the following instruction: "The students themselves would not think of such a delay in entering the work if it were not urged upon them by those who are supposed to be shepherds and guardians." This system was described as, "This long drawn out process, adding and adding more time, more branches." The Lord expressed His disfavor in these words, "The preparation of the students has been managed on the same principles as have the building operations. . . . God is calling, and has been calling for years for reform on these lines. . . While so much time is spent to put

a few through an exhaustive course of study, there are
many who are thirsting for the knowledge they could
get in a few months. One or two years would be considered a great blessing. . . *Give students a start,*
but do not feel it is your duty to carry them year after
year. It is their duty to get out into the field to work.
. . . The student should not permit himself *to be
bound down to any particular course of studies in-
volving long periods of time,* but should be guided in
such matters by the Spirit of God. . . I would warn
students not to advance one step in these lines,—not
even upon the advice of their instructors, or men
in positions of authority,—unless they have first
sought God individually with their hearts thrown open
to the Holy Spirit, and obtained His counsel concerning the contemplated course of study.

" Let every selfish desire to *distinguish yourselves*
be set aside. . . With many students the motive and
aim which caused them to enter school have gradually
been lost sight of and *an unholy ambition to secure a
high-class education* has led them to sacrifice the truth.
There are many who are crowding too many studies
into a limited period of time. . . I would advise restriction in following those methods of education
which imperil the soul and defeat the purpose for
which time and money are spent. Education is a
grand life work. . . After a period of time has been
devoted to study, let no one advise students to enter
again upon a line of study, but rather advise them to
enter upon the work for which they have been studying. Let them be advised to put into practice the
theories they have gained.   . . Those who are di-
recting the work of education are placing too large

an amount of study before those who have come to Battle Creek to fit up for the work of the Master. They have supposed it was necessary for them to go deeper and deeper into educational lines; and while they are pursuing various courses of study, year after year of precious time is passing away.

"The thought to be kept before students is that time is short and that they must make a speedy preparation for doing the work that is essential for this time. . . Understand that I say nothing in these words to depreciate education, but to warn those who are in danger of carrying that which is lawful to unlawful extremes." (T. E., pp. 105-146).

THE RESULTS OF FOLLOWING THIS PLAN of education is well illustrated by the experiences of Battle Creek College when it was working hard to follow the traditional courses leading to degrees which her faculty hoped would be looked upon with favor by the world. The following words show the danger from receiving such an education: "The Holy Spirit has often come to our schools, and has not been recognized, but has been treated as a stranger, perhaps as an intruder." "Again and again the heavenly messenger has been sent to the school." "The Great Teacher Himself was among you. How did you honor Him? Was He a stranger to some of the educators?" (T. E., pp. 51, 82, 203).

It is with shame and sadness that we are compelled to acknowledge that we teachers were as dead, spiritually, to the heavenly Teacher as were school men to the first angel before 1844. The greatest objection raised against the Holy Spirit instructing teachers as to the right ways of conducting the school at the time was that it would take students from their regular studies and disturb their plans for finishing a course and receiving degrees.

Much instruction was sent to the school on the subject of long and rigid courses, but the teachers and students of Battle Creek College, to a large extent, turned away from the instruction of the heavenly visitant. We must remember that Battle Creek College had not been established in the place that the Spirit directed. It did not follow the pattern for its establishment; it did not eve nattempt to introduce and practice the important educational reforms revealed by the Lord before 1844, but was content to get its ideas, life and inspiration from the colleges of those religious denominations that had rejected the first angel's message.

We have already read that "the customs and practices of the Battle Creek School go forth to all the churches, and the pulse heart beats of that school are felt throughout the body of believers." We must, therefore, conclude that as all the churches and believers were more or less under the influence of Battle Creek College at this time, at least a large per cent of Seventh-day Adventists would have treated the heavenly visitant, had He come to them suggesting reforms, as the Battle Creek College teachers and students treated Him. Perhaps, then, we can understand why God says, "The plan of the schools we shall establish in thes eclosing years of the work is to be of an entirely different order from those we have established. . . I have been shown that *in our educational work we are not to follow the methods that have been adopted in our older established schools.*

There is among us too much clinging to old customs, and because of this we are far behind where we should be in the development of the third angel's message." (Madison School, p. 29).

The founders of Battle Creek College made their mistake when they did not follow the plan given them by the Lord, but modeled the school after worldly schools about them. In these last days your test will come. You are not to pattern your schools after the older established Seventh-day Adventist schools, but are to follow the divine model. If we fail to understand this divine plan, we shall have no place in the loud cry.

REFORM CALLED FOR:—The teachers of Battle Creek College at that time received this word: "A succession of showers from the Living Waters has come to you at Battle Creek. . . Each shower was a consecrated inflowing of divine influence; but you did not recognize it as such. Instead of drinking copiously of the streams of salvation so freely offered through the influence of the Holy Spirit, you turned to common sewers, and tried to satisfy your soul thirst with the polluted waters of human science. The result has been parched hearts in the school and in the church. . . *But I hope the teachers have not yet passed the line where they are given over to hardness of heart and blindness of mind.* If they are again visited by the Holy Spirit I hope they will not call righteousness sin and sin righteousness. There is need of heart conversions among the teachers. *A genuine change of thoughts and methods of teaching is required* to place them where they will have a personal relation to a living Saviour. . . God will come near to the students because they are misled by the educators in whom they put confidence." (T. E., pp. 28, 29).

The instruction which came to Battle Creek College for years shows that during all those years the institution was unsettled on many of the important principles of ·Christian education. She was born with false ideas of education in her constitution, and she did not realize the source of her weakness. She was drinking from streams polluted more or less with worldly wisdom, but she did not know her danger. She was an educational germ carrier, and failed to realize that also. The straight testimonies sent to the institution must convince any believer in the testimonies that Battle Creek College was in great need of educational reform.

BATTLE CREEK COLLEGE MADE RADICAL REFORMS not long after these words were sent. It dropped the regular degree courses, and at the same time enriched the curriculum with a number of subjects very practical for the Seventh-day Adventist missionary, and "liberty in the choice of studies was regarded as fundamental." (Boone, p. 197). Each student, with the aid of the teachers, selected those studies considered most essential to his life work. The strength of the faculty was thrown heavily upon those subjects that had been neglected and for which God had been calling for years. When the school broke away from the stereotype courses and degrees, it found itself much more capable of following the instruction sent by the Lord, and the result was that in a short time Battle Creek College was planted on a beautiful farm. It was given an opportunity to get into an upright position, and then this most remarkable statement came: *"It is the beginning of the educational reform."* "No educational institution can place itself in opposition to the errors and corruptions of this degenerate age without receiving threats and insults, but time will place such an institution upon an elevated platform." (G. C. Bulletin, 1901, p. 454).

This subject has been treated so fully because some of you students question why we do not arrange studies in courses leading to degrees. You should know where you stand, and why you stand there, and should ask, "Am I following the plan instituted by Battle Creek College, which effected seriously every church in the denominaeion, or am I following that other plan of which the Lord said, "It is the beginning of educational reform?"

DEGREES AND WHAT THEY LEAD TO:—Degrees have been indirectly referred to, for they are the reward of the traditional courses. Were it not for the degree, it woud be impossible to hold most students to a prescribed course. However, the most dangerous element in degree granting does not seem to be comprehended by those Christian educators who cling to the custom. A degree is a sign or seal of authority. Ir the Christian church "the conferring of degrees was originated by a pope" as a sign of his authority over the educational system. Today degrees are conferred by the State, and the State has no right to set its seal to the work of an institution unless it can approve the system of education offered by that school. The degree is a sign of its approval. Any Seventh-day Adventist school that grants degrees, thereby invites State inspection, and must accept the world's standard and come into conformity to the worldly system of education. Claiming to conduct Christian schools, we yet seek to so teach that we can satisfy the worldly system. In time the State will either demand absolute conformity to her system or refuse to grant the degrees. If we are building up our work in such a manner as to encourage students to seek degrees, there is great danger that we will compromise on the true science of education in order to retain the State's seal or mark.

Seventh-day Adventists are not ignorant of the fact that even today the Papacy has the control practicaly of all education, and in a short time this will be openly avowed. Then the inspection of our degree granting schools will be done directly by the Papacy, and a degree, if granted, will again come directly from that organization. It will be a seal or a mark of the beast. Other Protestants failed here. What shall we Seventh-tay Adventist students do?

One educator has summed up the whole degree question as follows: "From his first introduction into the school, to the taking of his final degree, teachers, parents, and doting friends conspire in their efforts to stimulate the boy to get ahead of some one else. Men wear degrees as women wear fine bonnets, jewels in their hair, rings in their ears and on their fingers, and gay ribbons flaunting in the breeze. Consider, for example, the ornamental value of A. M., M. S., Ph. D., or the social value of such a tremendous decorative combination as that enjoyed by Mr. James Brown, A. M., Ph. D., LL. D., D. D. Each one of these titles costs as much as a diamond of moderate size, or a large pearl (not the Pearl of great price), and is worn for praceically the same reason. It does not necessarily indicate anything. John Smith, tailor; James Brown, blacksmith; Mr. Jones, surveyor, are examples of titles which produce in the mind some-thing more than the mere decorative effect. These indicate the trade or profession by which the man gains his livelihood."

Because the degree simply puts the possessor in a position which distinguishes him from those who do not hold one, and is not an indication of power to accomplish, worldly men who are building up an educational aristocracy feel that it is necessary to protect themselves by limiting the degree-conferring power. They say, "There should be legislation regulating the granting of academic degrees." The following extract from a report signed by a number of presidents of leading universities appeared in the columns of the *Educational Review*, "The degree conferring power is not to be granted to any institution having requirements for admission and for graduation lower than the minimum standard established by the commission, or to any institution whose productive endowment is not equal to at least $100,000.00. The law is an admirable one, and ought to be adopted by every state in the union in order that wild cat education may go the way of wild cat banking."

You will be interested in the following statement contained in a letter, written by the Educational Secretary of the Seventh-day Adventist denomination in 1896, concerning an interview with Mrs. E. G. White on this subject: "I explained to her the significance of the degrees and the meaning which was attached to them, and the general course of study which was implied by them in the eyes of other educators, and her idea seemed to be that there is no need that we should pay attention to these things; that what we want to do is to educate for usefulness here and the eternal kingdom hereafter; and that the question with our people is not whether a young man has a degree, but whether he has a suitable preparation so that he can be a blessing to others in this work. . . I should want to feel perfectly free to arrange the work just as I thought would be best for the young people and for the work, without being bound by the idea that you must maintain a course of study so that you can consistently grant degrees."

The object of our schools should be to prepare students to carry the message of Christ's second coming to all the world, and to prepare them speedily. "His work is not to wait while his servants go through such wonderfully elaborate preparations as our schools are planning to give." (T. E., p. 120).

Let us hope that Seventh-day Adventists may save themselves from those pitfalls that caught the Protestant denominations before 1844.

EDUCATIONAL PRINCIPLES.

"Before we carry the message of present truth in all its fullness to other counties, we must first break every yoke. *We must come into the line of true education,* walking in the wisdom of God, and not in the wisdom of the world. God calls for messengers who will be true reformers. We must educate, educate, to prepare a people who will understand the message, and then give the message to the world." (Madison School, p. 30). The object of these studies has been to aid you students to understand the instruction in the paragraph just read, that you may avoid the educational pitfalls, and that you may "come into the line of true education," and have a part in carrying the message to the world.

We shall review briefly the subject, and list important educational principles found in both systems. As these are presented, determine your attitude to each one, and ascertain your reason for taking that position. You are asked to do this with the hope that it will strengthen your position on educational questions, and aid you to "come into the line of true education," and thus be better prepared to carry the message of Christ's soon coming. It is done with the hope that you may more fully sense the deep significance of the statement, "Now as never before we need to understand the true science of education. If we fail to understand this, we shall never have a place in the kingdom of God."

1. Protestants hold their children in the church when they receive Christian education. They lose these children when they attend schools having a Pa-

pal system. Melancthon said, "Religion cannot be maintained without them (schools)."

2. The Papal system of education is never a fit model for Protestant schools. Luther and Melancthon recognized this. Accordingly they reformed the school system, changing the curriculum, text books, and methods of teaching.

3. Some schools, Christian in form, follow the Papal system, sandwiching in a little Bible, and flavoring the course with Protestant theology. John Sturm did this. So have some schools since the days of Sturm.

4. This combination educational system—Christian and Papal mixed—always opens the way for hairsplitting theological controversies, and the students are neglected for heresy hunting. It always terminates in a victory for Papacy over Protestantism.

5. The Papal system of education makes a Moloch of abstract subjects and worships at his shrine. Its strength lies in repeating meaningless forms, and "a dead study of words takes the place of a living knowledge of things." Mental cramming and formal memorizing are exalted methods of its teachers. Emulation, prizes and rewards are needed stimulants for "a mechanical and compulsory drill in unintelligible formulas," and their long stereotype courses end in degrees, the sign or mark of the system. It is the subjugation of human minds to the authority of some one above, the stifling of free thought by unnatural, close supervision in place of self-government. It leads away from nature, nature's work and nature's God, and centralizes in cities and man-made institutions. This is Papal education, and its reward is the

degree conferred at the end of the traditional course.

6. Every school is the pulse beat of some organization;—of the State, if it is a state school; of the Papacy, if a Papal school; and of the Christian church if it is a Christian school. Any educational system which mechanically teaches a stereotype course leading to degrees, will, in time, result in the development of a creed by its controlling organization—a creed written, or perhaps consisting only of the opinions of those in power, but a creed nevertheless, according to which every one not recognizing its power to initiate is considered irregular or independent.

7. Protestant education allows the student freedom in the choice of studies. This freedom from the stereotype course bears fruit in a church which provides for differences of opinion without the cry of heresy. Courses and degrees are an essential element in a religious trust. Trusts, in the very nature of things, can make no use of those who question their authority; those who differ must be crushed.

8. There are but two systems of education, one inspired by the Word of God and one by other literature. The Christian school not only has Bible study in its curriculum, but Bible principles are the guide of the student's life, and the spirit of the Bible is the inspiration of the school. If Bible principles are not the foundation of all subjects and the basis of all teaching, that school, even though Christian in name, has imbibed Papal principles. Oberlin, breaking from the Papal system before 1844, "restored the Bible to its place as a permanent text book," and pagan and infidel authors were thrown out.

9. Any system of education that exalts the Bible

will receive light on health reform, simplicity of dress, country life, etc. Oberlin, preparing for the midnight cry before 1844, accepted light on these subjects. Students discarded the use of flesh foods, tobacco, condiments, tea and coffee, rich pastries, hot breads, they used graham flour, discarded sloppy foods, expensive dress, jewelry, accepted the country as God's home for man, etc. These same reforms will be carried to completion by those who are preparing for the loud cry.

10. Christian schools are content with simple, modest buildings and equipment, but must give great and mighty truth. Papal schools must have massive buildings and elaborate equipment, but are content with little, or adulterated truth. Jefferson and others dealing with big truths caught the idea of simple buildings. The loud cry will be ushered in by schools content with simple buildings and equipment, but they will be doing a great work.

11. Christian education is not content with only learning things in the mind. What is studied must be put into practice. Manual training is a part of every Christian school curriculum. The Papal system is content to have its students learn and hold the knowledge without making any practical application. Its students are ever learning, but never able to come to a knowledge of the truth. Manual training is not an essential part of their education. Before 1844, reformers in education established many manual training schools where students were taught agriculture, horticulture, gardening, various trades, such as blacksmithing, carpentry, manufacture of cloth, printing, domestic science, dressmaking, care of the sick, etc.

They were breaking away from the Papacy, and were coming "into the line of true education." Since the loud cry will find many schools that have carried these reforms farther, the results will be greater.

12. Christian training schools make provision for physical culture and healthful exercise by providing plenty of useful labor. Papal education makes little provision for manual training, therefore athletics, sports, games and gymnasiums become the artificial substitutes for God's plan for physical exercises. Schools preparing students for the loud cry should complete the work they have started.

13. Christian schools have for one of their most important objects the training of students to be self-governing, to take their places, not as dependent and devitalized members of the church, but as indepndent and original workers, under the direction of God's Spirit, all co-operating in harmony with divine principles. The Papal system makes no effort to train students to be self-governing, for such a training is fatal to the Papal church organization. Self-government appeared as an integral part of educational reform before 1844. Is it appearing in your school?

14. Every Christian missionary should be a producer. In other words, he should be self-supporting. No great religious movement can be started, or successfully carried forward, that has not an army of lay members who are active self-supporting missionaries. Christian schools have no greater object than to train such an army. Papal schools must avoid this, for it is destructive to their system of organization for controlling men. Christian schools before 1844 caught this idea of training missionaries for the midnight

cry. Church leaders suppressed this reform. Christian schools before the loud cry will turn out an army of self-supporting workers.

15. The needy places of the world are calling for self-supporting missionaries. When the church opposed Oberlin's training missionaries, and refused to give them a place in the regular work, thousands of them went to the Indians, to the freedmen, to the mountain whites, and to foreign countries, under the direction of the American Missionary Society, an organization created by self-supporting workers.

16. Oberlin teachers, in order to make their school a success, sacrificed heavily in the matter of wages. Her students were encouraged to go where God called, with little concern over the qustion of remuneration. Oberlin considered it her duty as well as her pleasure to assist students to find their life work.

17. Oberlin teachers shortened the time students spent in school, and made their study practical by correlating class work with the reforms they desired their students to accept.

18. Opposition to Oberlin, while she was in the line of true education, brought to her friends and their means, and her attendance increased.

19. Outside opposition is a serious matter to a Christian school, but so long as the school keeps in "the line of true education," the opposition will only strengthen the reform. But long continued internal opposition is destructive. It was responsible for the downfall of the 16th century Reformation; it ruined the movement in 1844.

20. The spirt of a parent is necessary to the

prosperity and continued success of educational reforms. Oberlin had this blessing in a marked degree. Consider the advantage of having one teacher, strong as a reformer, on a faculty for fifty years.

Students, are you doing all you can to bring your school "into the line of true education?"

PRACTICAL SUBJECTS FOR THE CURRICULUM.

"The students are in our schools for a special training, to become acquainted with all lines of work, that, should they go out as missionaries, they could be self-reliant and able, through their educated ability, to furnish themselves with necessary conveniences and facilities." (T., Vol. 6, p. 208). "Studies should generally be few and well chosen, and those who attend our colleges are to have a different training than that of the common schools of the day." (C. E., p. 47).

In addition to those subjects usually considered essential, we have the following which our schools should teach, so that the student, leaving the institution, is equipped not only to teach them to others, but to use them for his own support:—

CARPENTRY AND BUILDING:—"Under the guidance of experienced carpenters . . . . students themselves should *erect buildings* on the school grounds . . . learning how to build economically." (T., Vol. 6, p. 176).

AGRICULTURE. FRUIT RAISING, GARDENING:— "Study in agricultural lines should be the A, B, C, of the education given in our schools. . . Small fruits should be planted, and vegetables and flowers cultivated. . . (Students) are to plant ornamental and fruit trees." (Idem, pp. 179, 182).   ,

VARIOUS TRADES:—"Preparation should be made for teaching blacksmithing, painting, shoemaking, cooking, baking, laundering, mending, typewriting and printing." (Idem, p. 182).

STOCK AND POULTRY RAISING:—"Students have been taught . . . to care wisely for cattle and poultry." (An Appeal for the Madison School).

NURSING:—"Training for medical missionary work is one of the grandest objects for which any school can be established." (Idem).

HOUSEHOLD DUTIES:—"Boys as well as girls should gain a knowledge of household duties. . . To make a bed and put a room in order, to wash dishes, to prepare a meal, to wash and repair his own clothing, is a training that need not make any boy less manly. . . Let girls, in turn, learn to harness and drive a horse, and to use the saw and hammer as well as the rake and the hoe." (Ed., p. 216).

COOKING AND SEWING:—"There should have been experienced teachers to give lessons to young ladies in the cooking department. Young girls should have been instructed to manufacture wearing apparel, to cut, make and mend garments." (C. E., p. 19).

SELF-SUPPORT:—Students "have been learning to become self-supporting, and a training more important than this they could not receive." "The lesson of self-help learned by the student would go far toward preserving institutions of learning from the burden of debt." (Ed., p. 221).

HAND WORK:—There is a science in hand work which Christian educators must recognize It is a brain developer as well as a way to physical support. Scientists have found that symmetrical mental development is impossible apart from this physical training, for by the use of the hand an important area of the brain is developed. Again, a time of trouble is ahead of us when those who are in "the line of true education" will not have access to machinery which is so common today, and much now done in factory and shop will of necessity be done by hand. But success in this as in every reform will be in proportion to one's love of the cause. The educator who spoke of manual training as "hoe-handle education" came from a school whose Board had provided facilities for teaching agriculture and various trades, but these had all been neglected. That teacher's attitude made the students feel that these important subjects were only secondary.

A CHANGED PROGRAM NECESSARY:—Many of the subjects in the curriculum, the Lord has said, are not essential and should be weeded out. These practical studies, he says, are essential, but they can not find their proper place by the side of the intellectual subjects until the program, followed for years and adapted to the old order, is radically changed to meet the new demands. Again, it is necessary to make a number of radical reforms before a program can be arranged which gives students an opportunity to earn their school expenses while studying. "We need schools that will be self-supporting, and this can be if teachers and students will be helpful, industrious and economical." (T. Jan. 24, 1907). We must have schools of this character to train the missionaries that God calls for in the loud cry.

SCHOOLS OF A NEW ORDER:—"The plan of the schools we shall establish in these closing years of the work are to be of an entirely different order from those we have instituted. . . There is among us too much clinging to old customs, and *because of this we are far behind where we should be in the development of the third angel's message.* Because men could not comprehend the purpose of God in the plans laid before us for the education of workers, methods have been followed in some of our schools which have retarded rather than advanced the work of God." (Madison School, p. 29).

In the school with the new order of things we shall find that in addition to other essential studies, "The students have been taught to raise their own crops, to build their own houses, and to care wisely for cattle and poultry. They have been learning to become self-supporting, and a training more important than this they could not receive. Thus they have obtained a valuable education for usefulness in missionary fields.

"To this is added the knowledge of how to treat the sick and to care for the injured. This training for medical missionary work is one of the grandest objects for which any school can be established. The educational work at the school and the sanitarium can go forward hand in hand. The instruction given at the school will benefit the patients, and the instruction given to the sanitarium patients will be a blessing to the school. . . The class of education given . . . . is such as will be accounted a treasure of great value by those who take up missionary work in foreign fields. If many more in other schools were receiving a similar training, we as a people would be a spectacle to the world, to angels, and to men. *The message*

*would be quickly carried to every country, and souls
now in darkness would be brought to the light.*

"The time is soon coming when God's people, because of persecution, will be scattered in many countries. Those who have received an all-round education will have great advantage wherever they are.
The Lord reveals divine wisdom in thus leading His
people to train all their faculties and capabilities for
the work of disseminating truth. . . You have no
time to lose. Satan will soon rise up to create hindrances; let the work go forward while it may. . .
Then the light of truth will be carried in a simple and
effective way, and *a great work will be accomplished
for the Master in a short time.* . . We are to learn
to be content with simple food and clothing, that we
may save much means to invest in the work of the
gospel." (An Appeal for the Madison School).

THERE IS HOPE:—It is your duty as students to
seek to discover what God's plan is for our schools,
and may this little history enable you to better understand the kind of education that existed in our older
schools so that you may avoid it. Let me impress you
again with the thought that you must seek God for
help to keep you from having worldly yokes of education placed on your necks, even by your teachers. Remember that God has said these pointed words to us
teachers and students: "We are in positive danger
of bringing into our educational work the customs and
fashions that prevail in the schools of the world."
(Madison School, p. 28).

We have spent years wandering in the wilderness
of worldly education. If we lack faith and courage
to enter into this reform, God will raise up men who

will do it. Already we know of worldly educators who look with favor upon the plan of education that has been delivered to us. For instance, the present United States Commissioner of Education, Doctor P. P. Claxton, like Horace Mann of old, is in sympathy with it; and, after visiting a number of schools that are striving to work out these reforms, he expressed to a company of teachers his appreciation of the system of education in the following words:

"I wish very much it were possible for me to be present at the meeting of teachers and nurses of the hill schools which you are holding this week. I am greatly interested in the work which these schools are doing. The work which you are doing at Madison is remarkable and worthy of high praise. If you succeed permanently in maintaining the school on its present basis, it can not fail to accomplish great good. The work which you are doing is highly practicable, and seems to me to be based on important fundamental principles of education. The same is true of the small schools which I visited, and I shall watch their progress with the greatest interest. I believe that you will succeed in accomplishing what you have in mind.

"All education must grow out of the life of the people educated. You and the teachers you are sending out are wisely recognizing this principle. In order to educate children, parents must be educated also. All real education must be education of the whole community, and it must take hold of the life which the people live, making them more intelligent about this life. It is difficult and practically impossible to attain better conditions until existing conditions are understood."

Have we the Caleb and Joshua spirit, and will we say, We are well able, by God's help, to build up a school "in the line of true education?" We must remember the promise that our schools "are prisoners of hope, and God will correct and enlighten them and bring them back to their upright position of distinction from the world." If we are willing and obedient, God will give us the victory we need.

"Let not managers, teachers or helpers swing back in their old customary way of letting their influence negative the very plans the Lord has presented as the best plan for the physical, mental and moral education of our youth. The Lord calls for steps in advance." (Dec. 27, 1901).

"Teachers, trust in God and go forward. My grace is sufficient for you, is the assurance of the great Teacher. Catch the inspiration of the words, and never, never talk doubt and unbelief. Be energetic. There is no half-service in pure and undefiled religion." (T. E., p. 30). "Before we can carry the message of present truth in all its fullness to other countries, we must first break every yoke. We must come into the line of true education, walking in the wisdom of God, and not in the wisdom of the world. God calls for messengers who will be true reformers. We must educate, educate, to prepare a people who will understand the message, and then give the message to the world. (Madison School, p. 30). "Now as never before we need to understand the true science of education. If we fail to understand this we shall never have a place in the kingdom of God."

References

Quoted as

Acts of the Apostles, Mrs. E. G. White..................Acts
Christian Education, Mrs. E. G. White..................C. E.
Education in the United States......................Boone
Education, Mrs. E. G. White...........................Ed.
Education in Georgia, Charles E. James..................Ga.
Great Controversy, Mrs. E. G. White................G. C.
History of the Popes...........................Von Ranke
History of Education.....................................Painter
Higher Education in Tennessee, Merriam..............Tenn.
Life of William Miller, White......................Miller
Life of Melancthon............................Melancthon
Life and Works of Horace Mann.....................Mann
Macau'ay's Bacon.....................................M. B.
Macauley's Von Ranke..............................M. R.
Testimony, Series B, No. 11..................Madison School
Oberlin, The Colony and the College..............Fairchild
Philosophy of Education.......................Rosencranz
Rise and Constitution of Universities................Laurie
Review and Herald..............................R. & H.
Special Testimonies on Education....................T. E.
Story of Oberlin, Leonard..........................Oberlin
Testimonies for the Church............................T.
Thomas Jefferson and the University of Virginia,
                            (Adams).........Jefferson
Unpublished Testimonies............................U. T.